CW00572545

The *Lucknow* COOKBOOK

.................................~.................................

CHAND SUR & SUNITA KOHLI

ALEPH

ALEPH

ALEPH BOOK COMPANY
An independent publishing firm
promoted by *Rupa Publications India*

First published in India in 2017 by
Aleph Book Company
7/16 Ansari Road, Daryaganj
New Delhi 110002

All photographs except those in the Introduction by
Jasmer Singh, courtesy K2India

The views and opinions expressed in this book are the
authors' own and the facts are as reported by them,
which have been verified to the extent possible, and
the publishers are not in any way liable for the same.

ISBN: 978-93-86021-60-1

1 3 5 7 9 10 8 6 4 2

Printed and bound in India by Replika Press Pvt. Ltd.

The
Lucknow
COOKBOOK

In memory of
my father, Inder Prakash Sur
(14.12.1914–3.3.1992),
a gentleman and an epicure
and
Kunwar Vishvjeet Singh of Kapurthala
(29.10.1946–6.8.2017),
an intellectual colossus and a gastronome
and
Kamal Chopra
(27.12.1946–12.8.2017),
resolute and brilliant

Contents

A Note About the Book

Lucknow has always been a city of refinement and its cuisine reflects these sensibilities. In many ways, Lucknow was considered the cultural capital of North India. It was here that the Urdu language was developed to near perfection. It was here, too, that the Lucknow Gharana of Kathak dance and the Bhatkhande Institute of classical music—both major institutions—were established. Art and architecture, particularly Indo-Saracenic architecture, flourished in this city built along the banks of the river Gomti. Architectural heritage is history written in stone. This is true of the many fine buildings that still exist in this city.

Most importantly, Lucknow was and still is a city known for its composite culture, its Ganga-Jamuni tehzeeb. The material manifestations of this syncretic culture and refinement, this tehzeeb, were symbolized in the combined use of gold (Ganga) and silver (Jamuna)—such as in silver objects, parts of which were gold washed, or in the use of gold and silver threads in Awadh's famous brocades woven in textile centres in Varanasi and Lucknow. The quintessence of this culture was an amalgamation of the finest of Hindu and Muslim thoughts and their mutual acceptance. This composite culture, of plurality and complexity, was also reflected in the easy acceptance of the varied cuisines of the various communities that resided in Lucknow.

My father had arrived in Lucknow in 1947, shortly after the Partition of India, to make a home in this city. Seventy years later we still call Lucknow our home town although most of us no longer live there. Lucknow has always been an accepting society—my parents were warmly welcomed by several old residents when they first moved here. The city's rich and varied cuisine is partly due to this easy acceptance of people and their cultures from other parts of India and of those who arrived from beyond its borders, as did my parents and a maternal aunt and her husband after they were compelled to leave Lahore and their home in Undivided India.

The culture of Lucknow, which my parents encountered in the late 1940s, was undoubtedly Muslim. But Lucknow was also home to communities of Hindus—Brahmins, Kshatriyas and Kayasthas—along with British residents who had stayed on post 1947, Anglo-Indians, Christians, Parsis and Bengalis. They had, for generations, resided in Lucknow. Sindhis and Punjabis were rather late entrants. Each community had its own food preferences and many different methods of cooking.

The samosa, in its present form, was invented in Lucknow. Today, it has become ubiquitous and is found the world over. Chaat also originated in Lucknow. Lucknow also has its own distinctive biryanis and pulaos, both non-vegetarian and vegetarian. It introduced the dum pukht style of cooking. Lucknow's cuisine was influenced by the cuisines that travelled down the Silk Road from Turkey, Persia, Afghanistan and then down to Quetta and Lahore, eventually finding their way to Lucknow. Many of the recipes in this cookbook are distilled from this rich culinary heritage.

The British presence in Lucknow had changed the eating habits among the elite. So most homes began to serve a desi lunch and an angrezi dinner. Among my mother's women friends, coffee parties became very popular, as did high teas. After the Carlton Hotel introduced its popular Sunday brunches, many families also started to serve brunches at home. Anglo-Indian food, where continental recipes were adapted to suit Indian tastes, has been the subject of a previous book by my mother—*Continental Cuisine for the Indian Palate*. That book has recipes of what we called 'angrezi khana'.

The recipes in this cookbook are quite distinctly Lucknowi, whose hallmark is food that is delectable to behold, is aromatic and delicate and is, most importantly, nutritious. Many recipes are the signature dishes of particular homes. This book is primarily about the food that was served in our homes and in the homes of our numerous friends, with all its seasonal variations. This cookbook needed to be written by my mother, a legendary cook, to complete the story of Lucknow's delicious and varied everyday cuisine. It is a privilege to be asked to co-author this book with her and to write an account of my parents' fractured histories. These are the histories that have produced the food we serve in our homes.

David Lowenthal, the American historian renowned for his work on heritage and spatial concepts of the past and the future, had famously pronounced that 'the past is a foreign country'. This cookbook, although palpable with nostalgia, selectively recaptures events and objects from the past that are a part of the intangible heritage of food and familial memories of gentler times. These are collective memories that conserve a sense of continuity, of belonging and of being rooted. I believe food engenders social and family harmony; it anchors us and connects us to the past, grounds us in the present and gives us a sense of identity and belonging. Our personal histories define us and I have chosen to define this partly through Lucknow's food traditions. The preparation of food is learnt by observation, it is a process of osmosis. In our family, all four generations are reasonably good cooks. This book documents the recipes that we have learnt from my mother and from our many friends in Lucknow.

One can certainly cook from this book, but one can also read through the recipes to get a glimpse of Lucknowi culture and of the lives behind these recipes. This is a book for cooks and for armchair cooks because, for people who really love food, it is a lens through which to view this particular world.

Sunita Kohli
New Delhi, 2017

Vatan Lost and Vatan Found: From Lahore to Lucknow

MY PARENTS' STORY

You are not a drop in the ocean.
You are the entire ocean in a drop.
—Rumi

My mother first came to Lucknow in 1948, although my father had visited the city shortly after Partition in 1947. My parents' families came from Undivided India, from across the border in what is now Pakistan. But, as Anita Desai stated in her introduction to Attia Hosain's *Sunlight on a Broken Column*, that classic of Muslim life in Lucknow: 'in India, the past never disappears'.

My mother was from Balochistan, although her family was originally from Multan. At some point they had migrated to Quetta. My father's family were Rajputs of the Sur-Chauhan clan and were from near Jaisalmer in Rajasthan. His family sanad (a charter or document issued by the Indian government) reveals that many generations earlier, his ancestors had been warlords, with mercenary armies of their own, fighting for wealth and plunder. Family lore recounts that his ancestors had once arranged the marriage of one of their sons to the daughter of the local chieftain of Jaisalmer. But instead of bringing a baraat, they brought an army and captured Jaisalmer. Apparently there were five brothers, who within the next few years were themselves thrown out of Jaisalmer—three of the brothers fled to Afghanistan, one somehow managed to return to Jaisalmer and one fled to Gujranwala. My father's family comes from the Gujranwala branch.

In later generations, my father's family had been closely associated with Maharaja Ranjit Singh's court. My father's grandfather was a state historian. Their family fortunes being closely linked to those of the court, when the British annexed Punjab after the demise of Maharaja Ranjit Singh in 1839, the fortunes of my father's ancestors also declined.

My father's family were all professionals—doctors, army officers, engineers or lawyers. My paternal grandfather was a doctor, as was

My mother, Chand Sur, at her engagement, 1945

my eldest uncle. My grandfather had made all four of his sons give up the honorific 'Kunwar' (prince), when they entered high school. As far as my grandfather was concerned using this title would be like the wolf in the Farsi story who went to the top of the hill and shouted, 'Pedram Sultan Booth'—my ancestors were kings!

My father was the second youngest of seven siblings and was orphaned at the age of fifteen. After his graduation, he was the first member of his immediate family to start a small business in Lahore. He had opened the first Philips showroom there and

moved into a house on Templeton Road before shifting to Lakshmi Mansions.

My maternal grandfather, Gangadhar Rajpal, had been a mechanical engineer in the North Western Railways. He was a highly intelligent man and when the railways denied him permission to pursue postgraduate studies in England, he chose to resign. Bravely, he went to England without a salary, taking with him his young wife, two sons and two daughters—my mother being the youngest then. That's how she ended up doing her kindergarten in England.

When my grandfather returned to India, he was persuaded to rejoin the railways and was given rapid promotions. After a brief stint in Assam, where the damp climate did not suit him, he was transferred to Sind and was in charge of the railway lines to the famous Sukkur Dam on the Indus. The North Western Railway was the strategic railroad of the North West Frontier Province. My grandfather rose to the highest position that an Indian engineer was allowed to attain under British rule. My two older aunts always spoke of their father's three-bedroom railway saloon car that had its own drawing and dining rooms with an attached kitchen. This saloon was assigned exclusively for my grandfather's use. They had liveried bearers and excellent railway cooks. They travelled extensively by train, all over the northwestern regions of India and also went several times to Persia on the Trans-Balochistan line. They travelled to Wazirabad, Multan, Sind, Hindu Bagh, Lahore, Peshawar, Murree, Attock and up to Chaman where there was an attempt to kidnap my three-year-old mother—all pink cheeked and auburn haired. My mother was the second oldest daughter in a family

My father, Inder Prakash Sur, in his early twenties

of eleven siblings. She had two half-brothers, seven sisters and a brother.

As my grandfather was constantly on the move, he sent his two oldest sons, my mother and her older sister to Wynberg Allen boarding school in Mussoorie. My mother started going there at the age of eight. From Quetta to Dehradun was a long train journey of three days and two nights, followed by a road trip up the hills to Mussoorie. The road ended at King Craig from where the children had to walk ten miles to school on the footpath. The food in the school was atrocious. My mother and her siblings always pined for the wonderful food they had at home or in the saloon car.

In Quetta, my grandfather had built his house on Lytton Road which was near the governor's house. Years later, at a small dinner at home in New Delhi for the new high commissioner of Pakistan, the very well-read Ashraf Qazi, and his charming wife, I introduced them to my mother who was then visiting from Lucknow. In the course of their conversation they discovered that they were both from Quetta. When my mother mentioned that her father's house had been on Lytton Road, they literally fell into each other's arms! Ashraf's grandfather's house was also on Lytton Road. They had been neighbours. For my mother, this was a connection to her childhood home.

Many years later, during my first long trip to Turkey in 1998, we had gone to Iznik to see the Green Mosque. There, in the centre of a roundabout, we saw an ancient milestone that indicated the number of miles to Constantinople and the number of miles to Multan.

My mother, Miss Mussoorie

Incredible, but we were on the ancient Silk Road that went from Istanbul to Xian in China. And in China, while on a visit to Xian to show our grandson Zohravar the amazing Terracotta Army of the third century BCE, we saw a sign which read, 'Xian—the end of Silk Road'.

It is this Silk Road which transported not only people and goods but also cuisines and recipes that were shared along this great trade route. All this is now part of our collective memory. The Yoghurt Soup of Lucknow had its roots in Istanbul; the original kebabs were from Persia; the use of pomegranates and dried fruit in Lucknow came from Afghanistan.

My parents with my father's brothers and their wives at
Mohammad Bagh Club, Lucknow.

My mother was married in Quetta in 1945. I was born in Lahore in December 1946. When Partition was announced, my parents were holidaying in Mussoorie and were staying at the Savoy. I, a baby of six months, was with them. My grandparents were in Quetta and visiting them then was their newly married daughter, my aunt Krishna, who was pregnant with her first child. My uncle Kishore was in Lahore.

News of the terrible atrocities, of murders and killings on both sides of the newly demarcated borders reached Quetta, Lahore and Mussoorie. My two eldest maternal uncles were then in Calcutta. They rushed to Delhi and got permission to charter a plane from Quetta. They managed to rescue my grandparents, aunts and several others and flew them to Delhi, but no one was allowed to carry any baggage.

My aunt Krishna always said, 'We left our homes as wealthy Indians and landed in Delhi as refugees, homeless and with no possessions.' The only thing they brought with them was their education and their value systems.

From Mussoorie my parents had come down to Delhi and stayed in one of the cottages that belonged to the Oberoi Maidens Hotel in Old Delhi. (Apparently, it was here that I took my first steps and it was here too that my first birthday was celebrated. My parents could not have foreseen that when I was in my thirties I would design the main restaurant and bar of the same Oberoi hotel and would also go on to design many of their other properties, particularly in Egypt. Life is cyclical!)

Soon my maternal grandparents managed to find a house to rent in Rajpur, a town north of Dehradun. As the house had no electricity or running water, it was cheap to rent and my grandfather had to house many family members.

My parents dancing at Mohammad Bagh Club with my mother's sister and her husband

My father did not like Delhi as a city to settle down in. But the memory of his only visit to Lucknow when he was a student had stayed with him. He told us that he had been enchanted by Lucknow—it was the only city that approximated Lahore, which was then called 'the Paris of the East', with its charm, culture and architecture.

While my mother went to stay with her parents in Rajpur, my father went to Lucknow to explore his prospects. This is when he wrote to my mother about his impressions of and experiences in Lucknow. The letter reads like a page from Samuel Pepys's diary, a chronicle of the social history of the times. It also reveals the circumstances of my mother's sisters, post the traumas of August 1947. Perhaps because my father did not come from a wealthy family, he was better able to adjust to their drastically changed circumstances as compared to his two brothers-in-law. He immediately showed his courage and grit in attempting to establish a new life in Lucknow. It was apparent that his concern was not only for himself, his wife and his baby (me), but also for the well-being of his extended family.

Excerpts from the letter are below:

18, Royal Hotel,
Lucknow
30th Oct. 1947

Chan My Darling,

I hope you reached Dehra Dun with Kishore [my uncle, married to Krishna, my mother's younger sister] on the 23rd or 24th inst. safely. I have requested you several times to keep me informed about you at least twice a week, but you don't do it [even] twice a month. You are definitely indifferent. This definitely annoys me & worries me. Tell me, should you not have written to me upon your arrival at Dehra Dun. You can't say you didn't get time to write one letter to me. This has disappointed me very much. Kindly expressly telegraph me about my Guddie's welfare. Urgent.

Kishore must have informed you that I left by air for Lucknow on the 21st inst. It was a very comfortable and novel experience to be up in the air. I was in Lucknow, exactly in 1½ hours. Kishore must have told you that I insured myself for this flight for £5,000, i.e. Rs 70,000.

Things have been very favourable here. Soon after my arrival negotiations commenced and ultimately I concluded the deal on the 27th inst. for a small sum. You will be glad to know that I have got a beautiful showroom without any key money [pagri]. But here, it should cost at least Rs 15,000. So this was the first big luck. I shall tell you the story about it when you come here. Re. a good flat or a bungalow, there is no chance to get it in the near future. But I don't mind, as I am very comfortable in this hotel. I pay Rs 360 p.m. This hotel is far better in <u>service & food</u> as compared to Cecil of Simla or Savoy of Mussoorie. We get chicken twice or thrice a week, fresh fish from the Gomati river every night for dinner and choicest vegetables. I have two good friends in the hotel. One is the Swiss manager and the other is a German steward. The latter is a very pleasant fellow and really looks after me. He is now waiting anxiously for you to come. This hotel gets its supply of milk, butter and cream from the Military Dairy Farm and is really of good quality…

…According to what Kishore told me, Ved's [my mother's older sister] case of delivery must have been over. What is the result? Bhabhi ji [my mother] must be busy looking after Ved. How is Krishna now? Hope better and also I hope by now she can eat normal light diet. I have decided that if she can take normal light diet, she must come with you on 15th inst. She will stay with us, and I am sure this change will do her very good. Here it is clean healthy air, very nice boiled vegetables and fish served in the hotel. Milk [is] really good for her and Guddi too, as it is from the Military Dairy Farm in sealed bottles. I have already arranged. I am also writing to Kishore about it at Delhi, and tell Krishna to be ready. She will spend a month with us here, and then I'll take you both and my Guddi to Calcutta by air for a week for X'Mas. It will be a good holiday for you refugees. We'll see All India Tennis matches, go to the sea (Diamond Harbour) in a motor launch or a steamer. I am sure, it will be an exciting trip for Krishna and a change from the refugee atmosphere at Dehra Dun (talking always of losses there), it will do her good mentally and physically which she needs...

Now a word about Lucknow. I like it immensely. People here are very courteous. It has a clean look and clean roads. Several government and other buildings are very imposing. Above all the city is very peaceful and life seems worth living after the experiences I had in Delhi. Thank God, I am out of it...

...Reply all questions asked carefully in this long and I am afraid boring letter to you. Give my Namaste to Pitaji & Bhabhi ji [my mother's parents] and Kishore's mother, & love to Ved and children.

My kisses to Guddi   Yours affly,
                                                        Inder

As it transpired, my parents went on to live in the Royal Hotel in Lucknow for three years. Eventually, they did manage to find a lovely bungalow to rent on Ashoka Road and much later moved to Newberry Road, which was adjacent to Butler Palace and quite close to the Lucknow Zoo. The only other family members to move to Lucknow were my aunt Krishna and her husband, Kishore. Their sons, Karan and Ravi, were yet to be born, as also my brother and sister, Ashok and Rekha.

It took my father almost two years to get permission to return to Lahore. Such permissions had become very difficult to obtain. He had lived in Lakshmi Mansions, a famous landmark of stylish apartments around a quadrangle. Riaz Khokar, a former Pakistani high commissioner to India, had once remarked to me that 'the best bachelors in Lahore lived there'. My father lived in number 39. He had interesting neighbours and friends. Diagonally below my father had lived Saadat Hasan Manto, the great Urdu writer whose incisive writings on

My mother in her forties

the Partition are now widely translated into many languages. My father had always been a voracious reader, as also my mother. My father strongly believed that the printed book would always be the central element of civilization. Immersive reading became a family habit, although today when I sit in my own library I often think of what Susan Sontag, the great literary heroine of my youth said: 'my library is an archive of longings'.

Lakshmi Mansions was my mother's first marital home. When my father went to Lahore after Partition, he had asked the new owners of the apartment if he could visit and take a few of his books and personal papers. He had known the new owners a little as they had belonged to the same club. He had gone to Lahore with only two small attaché cases as that was all that he could take back from a house that was still filled with his things.

My mother had only spent a year and a half in this home. She said that my father was the only man amongst his large circle of friends who used summer curtains and winter curtains! And he was paying the princely sum of Rs 40 to his excellent cook, in comparison to the cooks of other friends who received Rs 4 to Rs 15 per month. My father recalled that when he visited his flat in Lakshmi Mansions almost everything in it was the same, except that the photographs in his silver frames had been replaced. Fortunately, the new owners had not destroyed his papers, so amongst two bundles, he found some photographs which he took with him.

While he was going through his papers, the lady of the house offered him a cup of tea. It was only when my father saw the tea served to him in his monogrammed silver tea service did the realization hit him that he was in fact homeless! While sorting through the papers and deciding what to take back with him he had felt so exhausted and overcome that he lay down on what he thought was his bed. The lady came in shouting, 'What are you doing, Mr Sur? Why are you lying down on our bed?'

My mother and her sister, Krishna, at a Wild West party, with friends from Union Carbide and Burmah Shell

My father never returned to Lahore after this visit. I'm sure he would have loved to go back. Many years later, in 2012, I took my mother back to Lahore and we visited Lakshmi Mansions. The name still remains although the building has become somewhat decrepit. I do not think the best bachelors in town live there anymore! But it was a moving experience for my mother as it had been for my brother Ashok and my sister-in-law, Shuchi, two years earlier. My brother picked up a fistful of mud from the quadrangle and brought it back with him to Lucknow. He said that his eyes had welled up with tears because of the many stories that my father had recounted of this city which he had so dearly loved and had called his 'vatan'.

I was fortunate that my youngest daughter, Kohelika, an architect, and I were commissioned to convert an old Sikh haveli, which had belonged to one of Maharaja Ranjit Singh's noblemen, into a boutique hotel. This is in the old city of Lahore and the property faces two World Heritage sites—the Lahore Fort built by the Mughal emperor Akbar and the grand Badshahi Mosque.

The language and manners in Lahore have always reminded me

Family summer holidays in Mussoorie. (L-R) My aunts Krishna, Sharda, Shalli, my grandmother and my aunt Oma. (Seated) My aunt Ved and my mother with me aged 7.

of Lucknow, even though in Lahore they speak mostly in Punjabi, but a Punjabi full of Persian and Urdu words. My father, like many well-educated men of his generation, was conversant with Persian and Urdu. My mother spoke Pashto, Multani and Punjabi and although she could read and write in Urdu, her spoken Urdu was very anglicized.

The hospitality in Lahore is extraordinary and its food is legendary. There are some striking similarities to the cuisine of Lucknow. But one difference is that the cuisine of Lahore is more robust, in the tradition of the Punjab. The traditional cuisine in Lucknow is more refined, more aromatic, more aesthetically creative and it is served with a greater nazaakat (elegance).

This city of Lucknow, the 'capital of India's most populous state, Uttar Pradesh, which extends along the banks of the river Gomti was once the centre of a distinctive and highly sophisticated society', says Rosie Llewellyn-Jones. It was here that a unique composite culture, known as Ganga-Jamuni tehzeeb, which is syncretic and genuinely embraces both Hindu and Muslim traditions, was born. That intangible tehzeeb is tangibly symbolized in objects of silver with gold plating and in textiles woven in fine threads of gold and silver, as one sees in the many kamkhwabs (gold and silver brocades) created in cities such as Lucknow and Varanasi and in the traditional ghararas and shararas embroidered with gold and silver gota and mukaish work.

It is the culture of the nawabs of Lucknow that most permeates its lifestyle. Lucknow is well known for the richness and the variety of its cuisine. Its cuisine consists of elaborate dishes. Many of these are described in Salma Hussain's excellent book on Awadhi cuisine. Lucknow is also famous for its street food—both chaat and the ubiquitous samosa originated in this city. The city has always been culturally diverse and its flamboyant buildings, many in the Indo-Saracenic style, have reflected this multicultural style of living, as documented by Adity Chakravarti in *Rehaish,* her book on the homes of Lucknow. Sadly, many of these once gracious homes are dilapidated and need urgent conservation. Despite this they are evocative and genteel.

In the Awadhi dastarkhwan, a Persian term literally meaning a meticulously laid out ceremonial dining spread, one always sat on the floor, where beautifully embroidered dastarkhwans were spread on dhurries or white sheets. Sometimes this arrangement was spread on a takht, a low wooden table. With the growing influence of the British, the dastarkhwan, from the nineteenth century onwards, started being laid out on European-style dining tables, such as the solid high art deco one in our home in Lucknow.

Nowhere is the Ganga-Jamuni tehzeeb better illustrated than in our immediate family, in the marriage of my cousin Ravi to Seran, a Turkish Cypriot. They met at Columbia University in New York. He is a secular Hindu married to a secular Muslim and they live in New York City. Ravi continues to be pulled towards Indian art and architecture and aspires to collect Mughal and Ottoman pieces. Seran's eye and taste are peerless. They represent a perfect union of Hindu and Muslim cultures.

Lucknow is one city in India where Muslims and Hindus celebrated the same festivals and even worshipped at the same shrines. As Salma Hussain says, 'the city's *taraanah* (symphony) is created jointly by Hindus

My mother with her friends at a Lucknow high tea

and Muslims living happily alongside each other and sharing common interests and habits and speaking a common language. Lucknow has been the "melting pot" of various cultures— Hindu, Persian and British.' Till today, popular biryani shops often remain closed on Tuesdays and during Navaratri, when even most non-vegetarian Hindus in northern India eat shudh shakahari (pure vegetarian) food. It is still customary for Muslims and Hindus to exchange gifts of prepared delicacies during each other's major festivals. Our neighbour, the former Chief Justice of India, Justice Baig, who lived across us on Newberry Road, always sent us delicious seviyan or biryani at Eid. My parents always reciprocated at the time of Diwali. (It was another matter that my brother Ashok and I, were often caught raiding Justice Baig's huge mango orchards where they cross-bred different varieties of mangoes, and always forgiven.)

Lucknow had a high degree of refinement as compared to Delhi. It was known for its 'tehzeeb, tameez aur nafaasat (manners, etiquette and sophistication)'. It is in Lucknow that the Urdu language acquired its finesse and perfection. Lucknow was home to some of the most vibrant and artistic expressions of its time. The Lucknow gharana of Kathak became one of India's major classical dance forms. The culture of Lucknow has often been the subject of Indian cinema, including Satyajit Ray's *Shatranj ke Khiladi* and Muzaffar Ali's *Umrao Jaan*.

It was Asaf–ud–Daula, the fourth nawab, who moved the capital from Faizabad to Lucknow in the eighteenth century and made it a prosperous and glittering city. The symbol of two fishes was adopted as the crowning motif of the Lucknow region. As the capital of Awadh for many years, Faizabad became the cradle of art and culture, music and dance. Interestingly, in all of the renowned classical singer Begum Akhtar's old 78 rpm vinyl records, she would always sign off at the end of a thumri or a dadra as 'Akhtari Bai Faizabadi'. Years later, my sister Rekha Surya became Begum

My sister Rekha Surya with her guru, Begum Akhtar

Akhtar's last shagird (pupil). Begum Akhtar frequently visited our home along with her husband, the barrister Abbasi Saheb. She would sing or rather gungunao (hum) without any saaz (musical instruments). If my parents met Abbasi Saheb and Begum Akhtar at a function, he would often remark to my mother, 'Chand, when are you inviting me for your delicious Irish Stew?'

Under Nawab Asaf–ud–Daula, Lucknow and Awadh flourished. He was a relentless builder, a generous and sympathetic ruler and a passionate patron of the arts. He built the Bara Imambara with its intricate bhul-bhulaiyya (maze) and the adjacent mosque, primarily as a relief project to create employment for his subjects during the 1784 famine. It is during this period that, quite serendipitously, the dum pukht way of cooking was discovered and became the leitmotif of Lucknow cuisine.

Today, it is interesting to see that Lucknow cuisine, whether in homes or at great daawats (lavish meals), has seen a revival of many

My parents' second home in Mussoorie.
My father with his brother-in-law Kishore Trehan and his niece-in-law, Seran.

of its age-old gastronomic traditions. Lucknow has always had a vast
and interesting variety of food that has belonged to different cultures
and cuisines. Lucknow chefs took the best of these ideas, absorbed
them into their current cuisines and made it into a uniquely Lucknowi
experience.

Many people, including my family have, over the decades, made
Lucknow their home. We all belonged to different faiths and we each
came with our own version of social mores, culinary etiquette and
food preferences. But it all became absorbed, in the broadest sense,
into the cuisine of Lucknow, as we saw and savoured it in the homes
of our friends. For instance, our Parsi friends like the Kharases and
the Viccajees introduced us to the delights of dhansak and other
Parsi specialities which had their antecedents in Persia. Although the
majority of the great dishes of Lucknow's fabled cuisine belonged to
a sophisticated Muslim elite that is highly subtle and refined, many
dishes were influenced by Hindu families who were vegetarian but
who took inspiration from non-vegetarian dishes. Yet other dishes were
incorporated into Lucknow's cuisine from Anglo-Indian, Christian

and Eurasian tables. All of this was referred to as the angrezi khana of Lucknow. The best vegetable and mutton cutlets were served in that great Indo-Saracenic edifice, the Charbagh Railway Station, in their dining rooms, now all sadly defunct. Their range of 'puttins' (puddings) was vast and delicious.

My parents in many ways tried to recreate the lost world of Lahore, without being maudlin and without exhibiting any regrets about their lost home. Their strength came from their strong familial ties and the many friends that they eventually made in Lucknow, a city that had always welcomed the foreigner and people and cultures from other parts of India. In Jonathan Tucker's comprehensive and monumental history *The Silk Road: Art and History*, he has included maps that show direct connections between Turkey, Persia, Afghanistan, Quetta and Jaisalmer. It is interesting that the last two cities are integral to my parent's history. Tertiary trade routes went on to Mathura and Delhi. In Delhi, the food culture of the Silk Road was absorbed. It then metamorphosed in Lucknow into a cuisine that distinctly belongs to this city.

In Lucknow and in Mussoorie, where my parents had established their second home because of their strong past associations with that hill station, my father had built around him, a milieu of good friends, good books and good food. Together with his immediate and extended family long evenings would be spent in spirited discussions on books, history and world affairs. Our family are habitual cookbook readers. We discovered the first gastronomic novel ever written, *The Passionate Epicure* by Marcel Rouff (1924). We read dictionaries and atlases for sheer reading pleasure.

My parents were frequently invited to the homes of their friends. They reciprocated as they considered cooking and entertaining an expression of affectionate regard for their friends. My mother, when she first arrived in Lucknow, had never really cooked before, as she had spent most of her life in a boarding school in Mussoorie. But she had watched her mother cook during their holidays in Balochistan, or wherever else my grandfather was posted across the North West Frontier regions. Her mother was a superb cook. Once my parents were well settled

The last photograph of my parents in their home in Mussoorie, Diwali, 1991

in Lucknow, my father arranged for the head chef from Government House to come twice a week to teach my mother. That was really the beginning of my mother's passionate involvement with cooking. Her cooking style has always been simple and she favours nutritious food and ensures that she uses authentic and natural ingredients. Her dishes are well-presented.

I think I learnt to cook when my mother made cocktail snacks. Newspapers were spread on the dining table and devilled eggs, tiny burgers, shami kebabs, baked beans on toast and savoury tarts were prepared. Everything was always home-made. This was before the time of hummus and pita bread, gherkins and Heinz baked beans and any number of cocktail snacks that are today so easily available in stores.

The only items that were then available were condensed milk, Kraft cheese and Marmite. We grew up eating and drinking home-made food and snacks. Only double roti (bread) was bought from the market. The sole exception was in Mussoorie, a hill station well known for its bakeries. The pastrywalla would arrive with his pastries displayed in a tin trunk which would be balanced on his head as he went from house to house. His arrival was the high point of the day for several of us cousins staying with our grandparents during the long summer vacations. Choosing the one pastry that we were allowed to buy per day required much deliberation!

My parents became members of the Mohammed Bagh Club where they made many friends. In those days men wore tuxedos and white sharkskin ones in the summer. My parents often used to have their friends dining at home. They were very hospitable and their hospitality was equally well reciprocated. The table was always laden with great dishes from my mother's kitchen. My mother's table and menus unconsciously displayed a melding of cuisines from many communities that was characteristic of Lucknow.

My parents were fortunate in their friends. Their group of friends were not only from amongst the old residents of Lucknow, many belonging to old taluqdari families, but they also had many friends who were doctors and officers in the army. Lucknow had a large cantonment. People from many communities from all over India had made Lucknow their home—like Moti and Gulu Thadani who owned Lucknow's iconic cinema hall, the Mayfair. Some of our happiest childhood memories are of going to the cinema and eating chicken patties, lemon tarts and ice-cream sundaes at Kwality restaurant, whose entrance was from the Mayfair foyer. An iconic bookstore of Lucknow was Ram Advani Booksellers whose entrance was also from the Mayfair foyer. In fact, Darshi and Ram Advani had become good friends of my parents. My mother was constantly exchanging recipes with Darshi and buying cookbooks from their excellent shop. Lucknow also had a reasonably large group of expatriates—people who worked in companies like Burmah Shell or Union Carbide (this was much before the terrible tragedy in Bhopal).

Apart from lunches and dinners, Lucknow also had a great tradition of coffees and high teas. To this day, high teas are a great favourite of ours, as is evident from my cousin Ravi's letter at the end of the book.

My mother was a good bridge player and bridge parties always meant an array of the most delicious and delectable snacks that would be laid out almost like a buffet. Although my mother and my aunt Krishna were the only ones that played bridge, a bridge party in the house was eagerly anticipated by the rest of us. The snacks and cakes were always delicious.

*Celebrating my mother's 92nd birthday with my brother
Ashok, his wife, Shuchi, and my mother's granddaughters,
Suhelika and Suranya, Mussoorie, 2017.*

This book of recipes is all about the good food that we grew up with. It is about the food that we not only had in our own home but is also what was served in the homes of our friends. My mother is a skilled enough cook to invent dishes such as her simple but delightful Jalebi Pudding. She learnt recipes from her friends as also from books and magazines but, recipes received or read, prompt her to create new dishes that are an interpretation of her personality and a reflection of her taste. She is constantly inspired by cookbooks and my reasonably large collection of books on food is influenced by her love for them. However, her version of a particular recipe was always her own as she is always experimenting with food. I guess all good cooks have this particular talent. My mother is now in her nineties. I, too, am in the autumn of my life. To quote Attia Hosain, 'the strength of my roots is strong; it also causes pain, because it makes one a "stranger" everywhere in the deeper area of one's mind and spirit, except where one was born and brought up'. For me, that is Lucknow.

Kebabs

In the seventeenth century, the word kebab was introduced into the lexicon of culinary terms as kebap, a word of Turkic origin. The Pathans, Persians and Turkic warriors who descended into the Indo-Gangetic plains from Central Asia with their chunks of salted dry meat were allured by the scents of the countless herbs and spices that they encountered in Hindustan. From there on, the kebap was transformed into kebab.

Kebabs were prepared with many aromatic spices such as cumin seeds, cloves, cardamoms, peppercorns, ground gram lentils and raw papaya, which were added in different proportions for different kinds of meat. These expensive spices exuded divine aromas and were used for marinating the meat for that melt-in-the-mouth texture, with garnishes of dhania (fresh coriander) and pudina (mint) leaves.

Lucknow's two most famous kebabs are Gilawat ke Kebab and Kakori Kebab. They are made with a complex blend of spices, some of which are family secrets. Lucknow's most famous kebabchi's shop is Tunday ke Kebab. All the world descends on this shop in the Chowk area of Lucknow to savour its unique kebabs.

The delicate Gilawat ke Kebab (popularly known as Galouti kebab in Delhi) are flat, medium-sized patties made of finely ground and spiced minced meat fried in desi ghee. According to legend, these kebabs were created for Nawab Wajid Ali Shah by his rakabdars (chefs), when he lost all his teeth in his old age. The original version contained more than a hundred aromatic spices together with different flower essences.

The recipe for Gilawat ke Kebab is from our great family friend, Jimmy, the Raja of Jahangirabad. His palace kitchens, dating from 1810, continue to serve the finest Awadhi food in Lucknow. His palace is slated for conversion into a heritage hotel. He has already donated his Jahangirabad Fort for higher education, particularly for underprivileged communities. Jimmy is perhaps the only raja whose family has been in continuous residence in their own palace. Jahangirabad Palace is situated at one end of Hazratganj, the famous market street of Lucknow, named after the brave and beautiful Begum Hazrat Mahal, the wife of Wajid Ali Shah, the last nawab of Awadh. She fought the British herself after his defeat and subsequent exile to Calcutta.

Kakori Kebabs, on the other hand, were not an Awadhi delicacy, but specifically a speciality of Lucknow, a city that was the social and cultural epicentre of Awadh. Again, according to legend, it was invented by the Nawab of Kakori, a town near Lucknow, when a British bureaucrat offended the Nawab by complaining that the Shami Kebabs that were served at his dinner were coarse and hard to chew. Thereafter, the Nawab ordered his chefs to create a more refined version of this kebab and it became known as Kakori Kebab.

The Shami Kebabs served in our homes are my mother's speciality. The original recipe was given to her by her friend, Zubeida, Jimmy Jahangirabad's mother. Subsequently, she taught it to us and it is served often in our homes.

GILAWAT KE KEBAB

SERVES: 8   PREPARATION TIME: 1 HOUR

INGREDIENTS

Mutton	750 gms, minced thrice from lean gol boti
Raw papaya	6 tbsp, ground to a paste
Desi ghee	2 tbsp
Dhania (coriander) seeds	2 tsp
Jeera (cumin) seeds	1 tsp
Hari elaichi (green cardamom)	4 pods
Badi elaichi (black cardamom)	1 pod
Laal mirch (red chilli)	10 pieces, whole
Dalchini (cinnamon) powder	1 tsp
Javitri (mace)	½ tsp
Laung (cloves)	6 cloves
Jaiphal (nutmeg)	2 pieces
Besan (gram flour)	9 tbsp, roasted
Salt	to taste
Charcoal	2 pieces

METHOD

Grind the raw papaya into a fine paste.

Sauté the coriander and cumin seeds, green cardamom, black cardamom, red chillies, cinnamon, mace, nutmeg and 4 cloves in a pan on a low flame for about 5 minutes. Then grind into a fine paste. Mix in the minced mutton, salt and the raw papaya paste. Keep it aside to marinate for 1 hour.

Mix the gram flour and the rest of the ingredients except the 2 cloves, the ghee and the charcoal. Put the mixture in a large pan. Then put the burning charcoal, 2 cloves and a teaspoon of ghee in a small steel bowl and place it in the centre of the large pan. Cover the pan with a heavy lid for the smoking process and let it smoke for 30 minutes.

Divide this mixture into 12 equal portions and roll into a ball.

Then, using the palms of your hands, press it into round flat patties about half an inch in thickness.

Heat a frying pan on a low flame. Add the ghee and individually place the patties in it and shallow-fry them on both sides for 4 minutes each. Serve hot with onion rings.

KAKORI KEBAB

SERVES: 8   PREPARATION TIME: 1 HOUR

INGREDIENTS

Mutton	1 kg, minced from lean gol boti
Onion	¾ cup, chopped
Onion paste	¼ cup, browned
Kaccha papita (raw papaya)	¼ cup
Kaju (cashew nuts)	3 tbsp, ground to a paste
Garam masala* (ground spices)	1 tsp
Khus-khus (poppy seeds)	¼ cup, well washed
Kaali mirch (black peppercorn) powder	1 tsp
Laal mirch (red chilli) powder	1 tsp
Hari elaichi (green cardamom) powder	1 tsp
Laung (cloves)	½ tsp, powdered
Laal mirch (red chilli) powder	1 tsp
Kesar (saffron)	1 tsp, soaked in 1 tsp of warm milk
Kewra (screw pine) essence	2 drops
Besan (gram flour) roasted	7 tbsp
Butter	50 gms, melted for basting
Desi ghee	4 tsp

---

*A typical Indian version of garam masala powder consists of black and white peppercorns, cloves, cinnamon or cassia bark, mace (part of nutmeg), black and green cardamom pods, bay leaf and cumin seeds. As an alternative, use ready-made garam masala powder.

METHOD

Grind the mutton twice and then the third time, grind it with the desi ghee.

In a large flat metal platter, mix the mutton with all the ingredients, except the butter, and knead it well. Set it aside for half an hour. Then knead again.

Divide the mixture into 16 equal portions. With oiled palms, shape the meat portions evenly around the skewers, about 4–5 inches each. Place the skewers with the raw kebabs on a charcoal grill or over a low charcoal fire for about 5 minutes. Baste with butter and cook again for 4 minutes, rotating the skewers slowly so that the kebabs cook and brown evenly. Serve the kebabs hot with small onion rings and mint chutney (these are the subtle differences of garnishes between Delhi and Lucknow).

PASANDA KE KEBAB
(MUTTON SLICES ROASTED ON SKEWERS)

SERVES: 6   PREPARATION TIME: 3½ HOURS

INGREDIENTS

Mutton (raan)	½ kg, leg of mutton
Onions	¼ cup, chopped
Kaccha papita (raw papaya) paste	1 tsp
Adhrak (ginger)	2-inch piece, chopped
Lahsun (garlic)	10 cloves, chopped
Laung (cloves)	5 cloves
Hari elaichi (green cardamoms)	5 pods
Jeera (cumin) seeds	1 tsp
Jaiphal (nutmeg) powder	½ tsp
Kaali mirch (black peppercorns)	16 peppercorns
Khus-khus (poppy seeds)	1 tsp, washed (has to be washed thoroughly as poppy seeds have a lot of dust in them)
Dahi (yoghurt)	¾ cup
Laal mirch (red chilli) powder	1 tsp
Salt	1 tsp or to taste
Butter	for basting

METHOD

Cut the meat into slices approximately 3 inches long, 2 inches wide and ¾ inch thick. Cut these slices into halves without cutting through the meat, leaving it joined at the end. Open the cut halves to make a single strip of approximately 6-inch lengths. With the flat of a mutton cleaver, beat the strips and flatten them out.

In a grinder, mix together the raw papaya paste, onions, ginger, garlic, cloves, cardamoms, cumin seeds, nutmeg, peppercorns, poppy seeds and the yoghurt. Then add the red chilli powder and salt. Spread this mixture out on a flat metal plate, toss the strips of mutton into it and leave it to marinate for 3 hours.

To create a wavy line, pierce and weave the skewer in and out of each meat strip at regular intervals, running through the centre at four points. Place the skewers with the mutton over an open charcoal fire or a barbeque and roast for 10 minutes. When one side is cooked, baste with butter and roast again for another 5 minutes, so that all sides are well roasted. Serve hot with green chillies and onion rings.

PATEELE KE KEBAB

SERVES: 8   PREPARATION TIME: 1 HOUR

INGREDIENTS

Minced meat	1 kg, fat-free lean leg (gol boti), finely minced
Onions	6 medium, finely chopped
Dahi (yoghurt)	3 tbsp, beaten
Pudina (mint) leaves	½ cup, finely chopped
Hari mirch (green chilli)	9–12 chopped
Kaccha papita (raw papaya) paste	3 tbsp
Dhania (coriander) powder	2 tbsp
Hara dhania (coriander)	16 leaves, finely chopped
Khus-khus (poppy seeds)	1 tbsp, well washed
Besan (gram flour)	1½ cup, roasted
Saunf (fennel seeds)	2 tbsp
Jeera (cumin) seeds	1 tbsp
Sukhi laal mirch (dried red chillies)	6–7 medium-sized
Hari elaichi (green cardamom)	6 pods, ground
Kashmiri laal mirch (red chilli) powder	2 tsp (for the colour)
Laung (cloves)	6 cloves
Javitri (mace)	1 piece
Jaiphal (nutmeg)	½ piece, grated
Kewra (screw pine) essence	few drops
Water	½ cup
Sunflower oil	1–1½ cups
Desi ghee	4 tbsp
Salt	1 heaped tsp

METHOD

Wash the minced mutton and place it in a muslin cloth for 15 minutes to allow all the water to drain out. Grind the mince again.

On a tawa (griddle), lightly roast the coriander powder, poppy seeds, fennel seeds, cumin seeds and the cloves until they release an aroma. Then grind them to a fine powder.

Mix the raw papaya paste with the meat and let it marinate for 30 minutes. Grind the minced meat once again to a fine paste. Into the meat mixture add the roasted gram flour, chopped green chillies, ground green cardamom seeds, mace, nutmeg, coriander and mint leaves and the Kashmiri chilli powder. Let it marinate for an hour, so that the minced meat soaks in all the flavours.

Brown the chopped onions in desi ghee, remove from the fire and then grind with the yoghurt to a fine paste and add to the finely ground meat. Shape this ground meat into large balls. Then on a high flame, heat the oil and fry the kebabs until they turn golden brown, ensuring that the kebabs stay intact.

Take a heavy-bottomed pateela (cooking pot) and pour in the remaining oil from the fried kebabs into it. Add half a cup of water and a few drops of kewra to the oil. Then one by one, closely arrange the kebabs in the pateela. Cover with a lid and seal it with kneaded dough so that the steam does not escape.

On a low flame, let the kebabs dum cook* for 15–20 minutes. Open the sealed lid and gently transfer these soft kebabs from the pateela onto a flat serving dish. Some of the leftover oil may be poured over the kebabs. Serve hot, garnished with fried whole red chillies.

---

*Dum means slow-cooking in a sealed pot which locks in all the flavours and aromas of the various spices and condiments. This style of cooking originated in Lucknow during the great famine of the 1780s.

FISH KEBAB

MAKES: 20 KEBABS   PREPARATION TIME: 40 MINUTES

INGREDIENTS

Fish, preferably rohu (carp)/ Singhara (catfish)	500 gms, deboned
Aloo (potato)	1 medium, boiled and mashed
Egg white	1
White onion	1 small, finely chopped
White bread	1 slice, mashed with a little water
Hari mirch (green chilli)	2 deseeded, finely chopped
Hara dhania (coriander)	1 tbsp/5 leaves, finely chopped
Garam masala (ground spices)	1 tsp
Salt	1 tsp or to taste
Sunflower oil	4 tbsp

METHOD

To clean the fish, soak it in 1 tablespoon of vinegar or the juice of 1 lime for 15 minutes. Then wash the fish under clean running water.

In a steamer or double boiler, steam the fish for about 5 minutes. Then mash it using a fork. Add the potatoes and the white bread slice to the fish and mash them together again. Now mix in the coriander leaves, green chilli, egg white, onion, garam masala and salt. Divide the mixture equally and shape it into 20 small oblong kebabs.

Heat the oil in a frying pan and shallow-fry the kebabs until one side is golden brown. Then flip and brown it on the other side as well. Drain the excess oil on a paper towel. Serve hot with small onion rings or spring onion rings (when in season).

SHAMI KEBAB
(FLAT MUTTON PATTIES)

MAKES: 50 KEBABS   PREPARATION TIME: 1 HOUR

INGREDIENTS

Mutton	1 kg, finely ground/minced
Onions	1½ coarsely chopped
Adhrak (ginger) paste	2 tsp
Lahsun (garlic) paste	2 tsp
Laung (cloves)	10 cloves
Hari elaichi (green cardamom)	3 pods
Dalchini (cinnamon)	2 sticks
Dhania (coriander) powder	½ tsp
Kaali mirch (black peppercorn)	1 tbsp
Hari mirch (green chilli)	1 medium, deseeded
Garam masala (ground spices)	1 tbsp
Chana dal (split Bengal gram)	1 tbsp, soaked in water for 30 minutes
Masoor dal (split red lentils)	1 tbsp, soaked in water for 30 minutes
Egg whites	2, lightly beaten
Ghee	1 tbsp for cooking
Sunflower oil	1–2 tbsp
Salt	to taste
Hara dhania (coriander leaves)	1 small bunch (10-15) leaves, freshly chopped

Optional: Khus-khus (poppy seeds), 1 tsp washed well and soaked in water for 30 minutes can be used.

METHOD

In a kadhai (Indian wok), heat the ghee and fry half an onion. Then add the whole masalas and the soaked khus-khus (optional). Cook for a minute.

In a pressure cooker mix the minced mutton with the onions, ginger and garlic pastes, the soaked and drained dals and all the dry masalas except garam masala and salt to taste (the water from the minced meat will help cook the mix together). Cook for five whistles.

Let the minced mutton and the dals cook thoroughly until the water has completely absorbed. Then take it off the fire and let the mixture cool down.

Grind the cooked minced meat mixture into a smooth paste using a grindstone or an electric mixer. Add the chopped coriander, green chillies, egg whites and garam masala.

Then shape the mixture into medium-sized tikkis (patties). Shallow-fry the tikkis in oil in a non-stick frying pan or use sufficient oil in a regular pan so that the tikkis do not stick to the pan, frying 10 at a time. Serve hot with small raw onion rings along with fresh mint chutney (see page 206 under Chutneys).

Soups

Lucknow specializes in shorbas, which are prepared according to the seasons—Kaale Chane ka Shorba, Dal ka Shorba and Badaam ka Shorba are winter soups. The latter has been a favourite starter for prime ministerial banquets at Hyderabad House in New Delhi since the time of Pandit Jawaharlal Nehru, whose family belonged to Allahabad. Hot Yoghurt Soup (Garam Dahi ka Shorba) originated in Istanbul, and became part of the cuisine of Lucknow.

Broths and stocks play a major role when it comes to the preparation of soups. There is nothing more satisfying than a soup made from home-made chicken stock which has been infused with the fragrant aromas of spices and fresh ingredients that have simmered and cooked slowly on a stove. My mother's recipe for chicken stock is simple and easy to prepare. Once cooled, this stock can be refrigerated and frozen for days. This has been a solid staple in our homes, as it is the base for many recipes.

KAALE CHANE KA SHORBA
(BLACK CHICKPEA SOUP)

SERVES: 8   PREPARATION TIME: 30–35 MINUTES

INGREDIENTS

Kaala chana (whole black chickpeas)	250 gms
Tomatoes	4–5 large, made into a paste
Onions	5–6 large, finely chopped
Adhrak-lahsun (ginger-garlic) paste	1 tbsp
Dahi (curd)	50 gms
Haldi (turmeric) powder	1 tsp
Laal mirch (red chilli) powder	1 tsp
Dhania (coriander) powder	1 tsp
Garam masala (ground spices)	1 tbsp
Badi elaichi (black cardamom)	2 whole
Tejpatta (bay leaf)	2 leaves
Sunflower oil	4 tbsp
Fresh dhania (coriander)	handful
Salt	2 tsp

METHOD

Preparation of the Kaala Chana:

Soak the whole black chickpeas overnight or for four hours, then boil them with 1 tsp of salt and retain the water.

For the Tomato Paste:

Finely chop the tomatoes, put in a pan with 1 teaspoon of oil and let them simmer until the water is reduced to a paste consistency.

For the Shorba (Soup):

Heat the oil in a kadhai (Indian wok) and stir in the cardamom and bay leaves. Fry the onions until they turn brown. Put in the ginger and garlic paste, then add the prepared tomato paste with all the masalas and cook for 10 minutes until the oil rises to the top. Remove the excess oil.

On a low flame, boil the retained chana water. Then add the chanas and allow them to simmer for 5–7 minutes and then add the tomato masala. Gently pound half the chanas in the kadhai. Let the rest of the chanas remain whole. Remove from the fire and the shorba is ready to be served. Just before serving heat the shorba for 1 minute and add finely chopped coriander leaves.

MOONG AUR MASOOR DAL KA SHORBA
(LENTIL SOUP)

SERVES: 8   PREPARATION TIME: 1 HOUR

INGREDIENTS

Moong dal (green lentil)	½ cup
Masoor dal (red lentil)	½ cup
Onion	1 medium, chopped
Gajar (carrot)	1 diced
Adhrak-lahsun (ginger-garlic) paste	1 tsp
Vegetable/Chicken stock	1 cube
Kaali mirch (black peppercorn)	½ tsp, freshly ground
Pudina (mint)	5–7 leaves, finely chopped
Water	3 cups
Butter	½ tbsp
Lime juice	2 tbsp
Salt	1½ tsp

METHOD

Wash the lentils thoroughly. In a saucepan, add the lentils, onion, carrot, ginger and garlic paste and the water. Cook on a low flame until the lentils become tender. Remove from the flame and let the mixture cool. Then grind the lentils in a blender.

Pour the ground lentils back into the saucepan, add the vegetable or chicken stock cube (optional), the butter and the salt. Cook for another 5 minutes. Serve hot, sprinkled with black pepper and lime juice.

BADAAM KA SHORBA
(ALMOND SOUP)

SERVES: 6   PREPARATION TIME: 35 MINUTES

INGREDIENTS

Badaam (almonds)	¾ cup
Milk	1½ cups, warmed
Water	1½ cups, hot
Cornflour	¾ tsp, for thickening
Garam masala (ground spices)	¼ tsp
Kaali mirch (black pepper)	1 tsp or to taste
Butter	1 tbsp
Castor sugar	½ tsp
Salt	1 tsp or to taste
Badaam (almonds)	¼ cup, roasted and slivered, for garnishing

METHOD

Soak the almonds overnight and then peel them. Set aside ¼ cup for the garnish. Make a fine paste of the remaining almonds by slowly adding ½ a cup of milk by pounding in a mortar and pestle or in a grinder.

In a saucepan, heat the butter. On a low flame, melt the butter and then add ¾ teaspoon of the cornflour and mix it for 30 seconds, ensuring that the butter does not burn. Slowly add 1 cup of lukewarm milk, continuously stirring and not allowing any lumps to be formed. Do not allow the mixture to come to a boiling point.

Take the saucepan off the fire and add the almond and milk paste, mixing it well and continuously. Add the castor sugar. Then place the saucepan back on a medium flame and slowly mix in 1½ cups of hot water, until it comes to a boil. Reduce the flame and let the mixture simmer for 5 minutes. Finally add the garam masala, black pepper, sugar and salt.

Serve hot, preferably in individual soup bowls, garnished with the slivered almonds. If served from a soup tureen, serve the slivered almonds separately.

The Lucknow Cookbook

CARROT SOUP

SERVES: 8   PREPARATION TIME: 30 MINUTES

INGREDIENTS

Gajar (carrots)	1 kg, diced
Onion	2 large, coarsely chopped
Adhrak (ginger)	2-inch piece, freshly grated
Chicken/Vegetable stock	2 cups
Light cream	½ cup
Sunflower/Vegetable oil	2 tbsp
Salt	1½ tsp
Water	1½ cups
Fresh dhania (coriander)	12 leaves, for garnish
Croutons*	4 bread slices with the crusts removed

Note: Make a potli (bouquet garni) of 4 curry leaves, 4 coriander leaves, 1 inch of freshly chopped turmeric, 1 teaspoon roasted cumin, 1 teaspoon fenugreek seeds and 3 dried and broken red chillies.

METHOD

Heat the oil in a saucepan, add the chopped onions and fry until golden. Add the grated ginger and cook for 1 minute. Put in 1½ cups of water and add the stock and the salt and bring to a boil. Then add the bouquet garni with the carrots.

Reduce the flame, cover and let the mixture simmer until the carrots become tender. Remove from the fire and take out the bouquet garni. Blend the soup in small batches until it has a smooth texture. Mix in the light cream. Serve hot, decorated with freshly chopped coriander leaves.

---

*To make croutons, remove the crusts of the bread slices, cut the slices into ½-inch squares and fry in hot oil on a high flame until they become crisp.

CHILLED LITCHI AND APPLE SOUP

SERVES: 8   PREPARATION TIME: BEST PREPARED A DAY BEFORE
                             SERVING

INGREDIENTS

For the Soup:

Chicken stock	4 cups, strong
Onion	1 large, sliced
Adhrak (ginger)	2-inch piece, coarsely crushed
Laung (cloves)	4 coarsely crushed
Chakr phool (star anise)	1 coarsely crushed
Dalchini (cinnamon)	1–2-inch piece, coarsely crushed
Kaali mirch (peppercorns)	6 coarsely crushed
Lime	1 juiced

For the Lime Sorbet:

Limes	3 juiced
Sugar	1 tbsp
Any lime-based soda	2 bottles
Salt	a pinch

Before serving:

Apples	2 cups, cubed and sprinkled with a little lime juice
Litchis	2½ cups, freshly seeded or canned

METHOD

For the Soup:

Combine the stock, sliced onion, crushed spices and salt in a pan and bring to a boil over a high flame. Lower the flame and simmer for 20–30 minutes. Strain the mixture and let it cool. Mix in the lime juice and chill overnight.

For the Lime Sorbet:

Combine all the ingredients and stir until the sugar has dissolved. Pour into a container and freeze overnight.

Before Serving:

Chill the apples and litchis for 1 hour before serving.

Spoon them into 6–8 chilled soup bowls and pour in the chilled soup to fill half the bowls. Scrape out the sorbet with a fork and add a spoon into each soup bowl. Serve immediately.

PEANUT SOUP

SERVES: 6   PREPARATION TIME: 30 MINUTES

INGREDIENTS

Peanuts	½ cup, roasted
Crushed peanuts	¼ cup, for garnish
Peanut butter	2 tsp
Onion	1 medium, chopped
Potato	1 medium, peeled and chopped
Vegetable stock	4 cups
Coriander leaves	12 leaves, finely chopped
Lime juice and zest	1 tsp each
Black peppercorns	1 tsp, freshly ground
Peanut oil	1 tbsp
Salt/Sea salt	1 tsp or to taste

METHOD

Over a high flame, in a large saucepan add the peanut oil and the chopped onions. Sauté the onions for 6–8 minutes, until they turn golden brown. Add the potato, peanuts, peanut butter and stock and bring to a boil. Cover and simmer over a low flame for 20 minutes.

Allow the mixture to cool, then purée it in a blender. Transfer it back to the saucepan and add salt and pepper. Stir in the lime juice. Serve hot, spooning the soup into 4–6 bowls and garnishing with coriander, lime zest and a few crushed peanuts.

GARAM DAHI KA SHORBA
(HOT YOGHURT SOUP)

SERVES: 6   PREPARATION TIME: 40 MINUTES

INGREDIENTS

Dahi (yoghurt)	2 cups, beaten
Besan (gram flour)	3 tbsp, levelled
Lahsun (garlic) cloves	4 peeled and finely chopped
Adhrak (ginger)	1 tbsp, peeled and finely chopped or grated
Mooli (radish)	4 firm and trimmed
Karhi patta (curry leaves)	8 fresh leaves
Laal mirch (red chilli)	3 whole, dried
Hing (asafoetida)	1/8 tsp, ground
Kaali sarson (black mustard) seeds	1 tsp
Jeera (cumin) seeds	1 tsp
Dhania (coriander) seeds	1 tsp
Sugar	2 tsp
Kesar (saffron)	6 strands
Water	1½ cups
Salt	½ tsp
Oil	2 tsp

METHOD

Beat the yoghurt with a whisk or a fork.

In a saucepan, slowly add 1½ cups of water to the besan mixing it well. Add the sugar, salt and the whole radishes. Mix and pour into a pan. Bring to a boil, then on a slow flame, simmer uncovered for 10 minutes (if it becomes thick add some more water and cook for 5 more minutes). Remove the radishes and keep aside.

Heat the oil in a frying pan. First add the asafoetida, then the mustard seeds, cumin seeds and coriander seeds. When the mustard seeds start to sputter, add the curry leaves and red chillies. As soon as the chillies start darkening, add the chopped garlic and ginger. Stir until the garlic pieces brown a little. Then add the entire contents of the frying pan into the saucepan of soup. Simmer the soup for

5 minutes. Before serving, cut the radishes into small pieces and add to the soup. Serve hot, garnished with the saffron strands.

CHICKEN CORIANDER SOUP

SERVES: 6–8   PREPARATION TIME: 30 MINUTES

INGREDIENTS

Chicken stock	6 cups
Kaali mirch (black peppercorns)	6–8 freshly ground
Dhania (coriander) leaves	½ cup, well rinsed but not dried
Lahsun (garlic)	4 cloves, peeled and finely sliced
Olive oil (extra virgin)	2 tbsp
Salt	to taste

METHOD

Heat the chicken stock over a medium-high flame and season it with salt and pepper.

Meanwhile, combine the coriander, garlic, olive oil and salt in a blender. Add a little stock if necessary to blend into a smooth purée.

To serve, add a dollop of the purée into each bowl of the strong chicken stock.

CHICKEN STOCK

SERVES: 8–10   PREPARATION TIME: 1 HOUR

INGREDIENTS

Chicken wings	1 kg, cut into 3 to 4 pieces
Peanut oil	2 tbsp
Lemongrass	2 stalks, trimmed, roughly chopped and bruised with the back of a knife
Onions	2 medium, peeled and chopped
Carrots	2, peeled and chopped

Spring onions/Scallions	6, trimmed and roughly chopped
Celery	½ a stalk with the leaves, trimmed and roughly chopped
Adhrak (ginger)	4-inch piece, peeled and roughly chopped
Lahsun (garlic)	10–12 cloves, peeled and roughly chopped
Garlic head	1 whole, cut into 2 halves
Red/black peppercorns	1 tbsp
Laung (cloves)	3–4 cloves
Dalchini (cinnamon)	1-inch stick
Tejpatta (bay leaf)	2 leaves
Salt	1 tbsp

METHOD

Preheat the oven to its maximum temperature (550°F/300°C).

Combine the chicken wings and peanut oil in a roasting pan just large enough to hold the chicken in one layer. Roast for about 45 minutes on the lowest rack of the oven, stirring and scraping the bottom of the pan occasionally, until the meat is richly browned. Add the vegetables and seasonings and stir once or twice. Then return to the oven for approximately 20 minutes more, stirring occasionally.

Carefully place the pan on top of the stove and add 6 cups of water. Bring to a boil over a medium flame and cook for another 30 minutes, stirring occasionally. Cool slightly, then strain.

Refrigerate. The fat may be skimmed after the stock cools completely. Reheat and re-refrigerate to remove more fat. Consume within three days.

Potatoes

Potatoes are commonly found in every Indian household, cooked in a myriad different ways. But Lucknow is known for its potato specialities. Being the most versatile of vegetables makes potatoes a saving grace for all vegetarians. Every time one was confused as to what to make for a meal, a new potato recipe was created. We had our house specialities like Til ka Aloo, Amras aur Aloo ka Saalan, Hing Jeere ke Aloo and Dahiwaley Aloo that everyone relished.

TIL KA ALOO
(POTATOES WITH SESAME SEEDS)

SERVES: 8   PREPARATION TIME: 1 HOUR

INGREDIENTS

Aloo (potatoes)	1 kg, small, even-sized
Adhrak-lahsun (ginger-garlic) paste	1 tbsp
Safed til (white sesame seeds)	100 gms
Besan (gram flour)	1 tbsp
Haldi (turmeric) powder	½ tsp
Laal mirch (red chilli) powder	1 tsp
Dhania (coriander) powder	1 tbsp
Amchoor (dried raw mango) powder	1 tsp
Anaardana (pomegranate seeds)	1 tbsp, finely ground
Egg	2 egg whites
Sunflower oil	4 tbsp, for frying
Kaala namak (rock salt) powder	1 tsp
Salt	1 tsp

Preparation: Wash the potatoes thoroughly, soak in water with 1 tsp salt for half an hour, then parboil the unpeeled potatoes and let them cool.

METHOD

Blend the besan, egg whites and all the masalas together into a paste. Put the washed and unpeeled whole potatoes in the ready masala, making sure that the potatoes are properly covered with the masala. Then generously sprinkle the sesame seeds on the potatoes.

In a large frying pan, heat the oil and fry the potatoes until they turn golden brown. Sprinkle rock salt and mix. Til ka Aloo is ready to be served.

AMRAS AUR ALOO KA SAALAN
(MANGO AND POTATO CURRY)

SERVES: 8   PREPARATION TIME: 40 MINUTES

INGREDIENTS

Aloo (potatoes)	½ kg, medium-sized, boiled and quartered
Aam (ripe mangoes)	1½ cups, pulped
Onions	3 medium, finely chopped
Dahi (yoghurt)	1 cup, gently beaten
Hari mirch (green chillies)	4 slit, deseeded
Adhrak (ginger) paste	½ tsp
Lahsun (garlic) paste	1 tsp
Haldi (turmeric) powder	¼ tsp
Laal mirch (red chilli) powder	1 tsp
Laung (cloves)	2 pods
Hari elaichi (green cardamom)	2 pods
Shahi jeera (black cumin) seeds	¼ tsp
Magaz (musk melon and watermelon) seeds	1 tsp each, ground
Kesar (saffron)	6 strands
Fresh cream	2 tbsp
Oil	1–1½ cups
Salt	to taste

METHOD

Fry the potatoes in a saucepan until golden brown and keep aside.
Reheat the oil and sauté the cloves, green cardamom and black cumin
for a minute. Add the onions and fry until they turn golden brown.
Then add the ginger and garlic paste, turmeric and red chilli powder
and sauté for a minute. Add the fried potatoes to this mixture and mix
for a couple of minutes. Add the yoghurt and the ground musk melon
and watermelon seeds.

Cook for 5 minutes over a medium flame, stirring continuously
until it comes to a boil. Then on a low flame, partially cover the
saucepan and let it simmer so that the water content reduces. After

the yoghurt mixture is cooked, add the whole green chillies, then add the lightly beaten mango pulp, the fresh cream and the saffron strands. Cook for a minute or two and remove from the fire. Serve hot.

KHATTE ALOO
(TANGY POTATOES)

SERVES: 8   PREPARATION TIME: 20 MINUTES

INGREDIENTS

Aloo (potatoes)	1 kg, small and even-sized, boiled and peeled
Jeera (cumin) seeds	½ tbsp, roasted and powdered
Kaali mirch (black pepper)	1 tsp, crushed
Laal mirch (red chillies)	1 tbsp, crushed
Rye	1 tsp, powdered
Dhania (coriander)	½ bunch, finely chopped
Hari mirch (green chillies)	3 finely chopped
Pudina (mint)	½ bunch, finely chopped
Imli (tamarind) water	1 cup, thick juice
Limes	2, juiced
Sugar	1 tsp
Salt	1 tsp or to taste
Sunflower oil	1 cup

METHOD

Heat the oil in a kadhai and deep-fry the potatoes until they turn golden brown. Keep aside.

On a medium flame, transfer the remaining oil from the kadhai into a frying pan and add the potatoes with all the ingredients. Shallow-fry the potatoes for 5 minutes. Cover the pan and let the potatoes simmer for 10 minutes on a low flame. Serve hot.

HING JEERE KE ALOO
(SPICED POTATOES)

SERVES: 8   PREPARATION TIME: 20 MINUTES

INGREDIENTS

Aloo (baby potatoes)	½ kg, even-sized and unpeeled
Adhrak (ginger)	¾-inch piece, chopped
Jeera (cumin) seeds	2½ tsp
Hing (asafoetida)	1 tsp
Hari mirch (green chilli)	4 deseeded and chopped
Anaardana (pomegranate) powder	1 tbsp
Laal mirch (red chilli) powder	1 tsp
Haldi (turmeric) powder	1 tsp
Salt	1 tsp or to taste
Desi ghee	2 tbsp

METHOD

In a saucepan, boil the potatoes in salted water for about 10 minutes. Drain, remove and keep aside. In the saucepan, heat the ghee and add the asafoetida and stir it in on a medium flame for 2 minutes. Then add the cumin and stir until the mixture starts to sputter.

To this mixture, add the ginger and green chillies and stir for 30 seconds. Add the potatoes and fry for 1 minute. Add the pomegranate, red chilli and turmeric powders and fry until the masala turns brown and evenly coats the potatoes. Temper the potatoes the desi ghee, 5 whole dried red chillies and ½ teaspoon of turmeric. Serve hot.

DAHIWALE ALOO
(POTATOES COOKED IN YOGHURT)

SERVES: 4   PREPARATION TIME: 30 MINUTES

INGREDIENTS

Baby aloo (potatoes)	½ kg, washed, unpeeled and boiled
Dahi (yoghurt)	4 tbsp, full-cream
Water	2 tbsp
Hara dhania (coriander)	12 leaves, finely chopped
Adhrak-lahsun (ginger-garlic) paste	1 tbsp
Laal mirch (red chilli) paste	1 tsp
Jeera (cumin) powder	¼ tsp
Dhania (coriander) powder	¼ tsp
Sunflower/Vegetable oil	2 tbsp
Nimbu (lime)	1 juiced
Salt	1 tsp or to taste

METHOD

Mix the yoghurt with water. In a heavy-bottomed pan, mix the boiled potatoes with the rest of the ingredients (except the lemon juice) and half of the yoghurt and water mixture. Cook on a medium flame until the oil floats on top and the spices are well cooked.

Then add the remaining yoghurt and cook until the yoghurt and spices start to stick to the potatoes. Serve hot with a generous squeeze of lime juice.

ALOO SALAD ANARKALI
(POTATO AND POMEGRANATE SALAD)

SERVES: 8   PREPARATION TIME: 15 MINUTES

INGREDIENTS

Baby aloo (potatoes)	1 kg, boiled and peeled, cut in halves
Kaala chana (black chickpeas)	1 cup, soaked overnight and boiled in salted water
Fresh anaar (pomegranate) seeds	1 cup
Anaardana (pomegranate) powder	1 tbsp
Amchoor (dry mango) powder	1 tbsp
Jeera (cumin) powder	2 tsp
Lime juice	5 tbsp
Kaala namak (rock salt)	2 tsp, ground
Peanut oil	3 tbsp
Salt	to taste

METHOD

In a small saucepan, on a low flame, heat the oil and add all the powdered spices to it. Sauté and remove from the flame. Let it cool.

Mix the potatoes and the black chickpeas with the fresh pomegranate seeds. Pour the lime juice and the ground rock salt over it and mix. Keep it cool at room temperature. When serving, mix in finely chopped coriander leaves with 2 tablespoons of the pomegranate seeds. The salad is ready to be served.

Vegetables

The most popular vegetables in Lucknow are torai (ridge gourd), lauki (bottle gourd), karela (bitter gourd) and arbi (colocasia/taro root). The majority of Muslim households seldom cook vegetables on their own—they are always added to their non-vegetarian recipes. But some sabzis, such as stuffed bitter gourd and okra, are cooked individually. Kathal (jackfruit) ki Sabzi is cooked by vegetarians with the same spices as bhuna hua gosht (roasted mutton) and closely approximates it in taste and texture. A great Lucknow speciality is Dabi Arbi ka Saalan. The arbi recipe is from the house of Mahmudabad. Suleiman Mahmudabad, the first convener of the Indian National Trust for Art and Cultural Heritage in Lucknow who, along with his sons Ali and Amir, both historians, are working to preserve the traditions of Awadhi and Mahmudabadi cuisine. They are doing this with the help of their family chefs who have served them through eight generations.

BHARWAAN KARELA WITH MASALA
(STUFFED BITTER GOURD)

SERVES: 8   PREPARATION TIME: 40 MINUTES

INGREDIENTS

Karela (bitter gourd)	1 kg, medium, even-sized
Onions	4 medium, diced
Dhania (coriander) powder	3 tsp
Garam masala (ground spices)	1 tbsp
Haldi (turmeric) powder	1 tsp
Laal mirch (red chilli) powder	1 tsp
Sukhi laal mirch (dry red chilli) seeds	1 tsp
Gur (jaggery)	2½ tbsp
Amchoor (raw mango) powder	1 tbsp
Panch phoron masala*	2 tbsp
Ajwain (caraway) seeds	1 tbsp
Sabut dhania (whole coriander) seeds	1 tbsp
Jeera (cumin) seeds	1 tsp
Oil	1 cup
Salt	1 ½ tbsp

METHOD

Peel the karelas and slit them along their lengths keeping both ends intact, deseed and then immerse them in warm water with a tablespoon of salt. After bringing to a boil, drain and set aside to cool.

In a kadhai (Indian wok) add a little oil and fry the onions until they turn slightly pink. Then add the coriander, turmeric and red chilli powders, dried red chilli seeds, garam masala, caraway seeds, raw mango powder, coriander seeds, cumin seeds, jaggery and salt. Sauté for 2–3 minutes until the jaggery melts. Add the panch phoron masala. Remove from the flame and let it cool.

Once the masala has cooled, stuff the karelas with it. Then shallow-fry the karelas in a non-stick pan until they turn golden brown. Serve them laid out on a flat serving dish.

---

*Panch phoron masala consists of, in equal parts, methi (fenugreek) seeds, kalonji or nigella (black onion) seeds, jeera (cumin) seeds, rye (black mustard) seeds and saunf (fennel) seeds.

BHARWAAN KARELA WITH ALOO
(STUFFED BITTER GOURD WITH POTATOES)

SERVES: 8   PREPARATION TIME: 40 MINUTES

INGREDIENTS

Karela (bitter gourd)	1 kg, small, even-sized
Onion	1 medium, diced
Tomato	1 large, grated
Aloo (potatoes)	4 medium, boiled and mashed
Karhi patta (curry leaves)	10–12 small leaves
Dhania (coriander) powder	1 tbsp
Garam masala (ground spices)	1 tbsp
Haldi (turmeric) powder	1 tsp
Laal mirch (red chilli) powder	1 tsp
Amchoor (raw mango) powder	1 tsp
Panch phoron masala	1 tsp
Oil	1 cup
Salt	1 tsp or to taste

METHOD

Peel the karelas and slit them along their lengths keeping both ends intact, deseed and then immerse them in warm water with a tablespoon of salt. Bring to a boil, then drain and set aside to cool.

In a kadhai heat the oil, add the panch phoron masala until it crackles, then add the curry leaves and finally the onions and fry them until they turn slightly pink. Add the tomato and mix well. Then put in the coriander, turmeric, red chilli, garam masala and raw mango powders with the salt. Sauté for 5 minutes. Add the boiled and mashed potatoes to this masala mixture and lightly brown them, remove from the flame and let them cool.

Stuff the karelas with the masala. In a non-stick pan, shallow-fry them until they turn golden brown. Serve them laid out on a flat serving dish in a single layer.

DUDHIYA TORAI/LAUKI
(RIDGE/BOTTLE GOURD COOKED IN MILK)

SERVES: 8   PREPARATION TIME: 30 MINUTES

INGREDIENTS

Torai (ridge gourd)*	1½ kg, peeled
Onion	1 medium, finely chopped
Tomatoes	2 large, grated and the skins removed
Hari mirch (green chilli)	3 medium, whole
Dhania (coriander) leaves	10-12 leaves
Adhrak-lahsun (ginger-garlic) paste	1 tsp each
Milk	2½ cups
Dhania (coriander) powder	1 tbsp
Garam masala (ground spices)	1 tbsp
Laal mirch (red chilli) powder	1 tsp
Haldi (turmeric) powder	1 tsp
Sabzi (vegetable) masala	1 tbsp
Oil	1 tbsp
Salt	1 tsp or to taste

METHOD

Wash the ridge gourd and dice it into small squares. Sauté the onions in oil and then add the ginger and garlic paste. Add the grated tomatoes to the onions and cook for 2 minutes. Now add all the masalas together. Brown this mixture well, until the oil rises to the surface.

Add the washed gourd to this mixture and sauté it. On a low flame, add the milk and cook for 30 minutes, until all the milk is absorbed into the torai. Finally add the freshly chopped coriander leaves and the 3 whole green chillies with salt. Cook for a minute. Serve hot.

---

*To make Dudhiya Lauki use 750 grams. The ingredients and the method are the same as for the Torai (Ridge Gourd).

DABI ARBI KA SAALAN
(FLATTENED TARO ROOT/COLOCASIA IN GRAVY)

SERVES: 8   PREPARATION TIME: 35 MINUTES

INGREDIENTS

Arbi (colocasia/taro root)	24, 2 inches long each
Vegetable oil	for deep-frying

For the Potli (bouquet garni):
Take a small handkerchief-sized muslin cloth. Place the ingredients below in it and tie firmly with a thread.

Laung (cloves)	8 cloves
Hari elaichi (green cardamom)	4 pods
Badi elaichi (black cardamom)	2 pods
Jaiphal (nutmeg)	¼ tsp
Khus ki jarh (vetiver root)	6 blades
Javitri (mace)	2 blades

For the gravy:

Ghee	¼ cup
Onions	¼ cup, thinly sliced
Lahsun (garlic) paste	1 tsp
Adhrak (ginger) paste	¼ tsp
Dhania (coriander) powder	1½ tsp
Haldi (turmeric) powder	1 tsp
Laal mirch (red chilli) powder	½ tsp
Kaju (cashew) paste	2 tbsp
Dahi (yoghurt)	2 tbsp
Vegetable stock	3 cups
Kaali mirch (black pepper) powder	¾ tsp
Hari elaichi (green cardamom) powder	2 tsp
Badi elaichi (black cardamom) powder	1 tsp
Nutmeg powder	1 tsp
Ittar (aromatic essential oil)	2 drops
Salt	1 tsp or to taste

METHOD

Boil the arbi (colocasia) until slightly soft. Drain, cool and peel. Then place it on a muslin cloth, fold it over and press to flatten. Heat sufficient oil in a kadhai to deep-fry the colocasia over a medium flame until golden in colour.

For the Gravy:

Heat the ghee in a pan. Stir-fry half the sliced onions until golden. Drain and remove. In the same oil, fry the remaining onions until translucent. Add the ginger and garlic pastes and stir-fry for a minute. Put in the potli and the powdered spices.

Stir-fry until the oil leaves the sides. Remove the pan from the flame, stir in the yoghurt, return the pan to the stove and stir-fry until the oil leaves the sides again. Add the vegetable stock and bring to a boil. Reduce the heat to a low flame and let it simmer, stirring occasionally for 30 minutes (the gravy should be reduced to half the quantity by then).

Add the fried arbi, bring to a boil, reduce the heat and let it simmer for about three minutes with salt. Remove the potli. Add the cashew paste and stir in the ittar. Serve hot.

KAJU KA SAALAN
(CASHEW NUT CURRY)

SERVES: 6–8   PREPARATION TIME: 40 MINUTES

INGREDIENTS

Kaju (cashew nuts)	250 gms, raw
Hara pyaaz (spring onions)	6, fully sliced
Hari mirch (green chilli)	4, 1 deseeded and thinly sliced and 3 whole
Lahsun (garlic)	2 cloves
Adhrak (ginger)	2-inch piece, julienned
Karhi patta (curry leaves)	6 small leaves
Lemongrass	2 2-inch pieces

Dhania (coriander) powder	1 tbsp
Haldi (turmeric) powder	½ tbsp
Water	1½ cups
Coconut milk	1 cup
Yoghurt	2 tbsp
Desi ghee	1 tbsp
Salt	1 tbsp
Dhania (coriander) leaves	2 tbsp, finely chopped

METHOD

Soak the cashew nuts overnight. Change the water twice or thrice to whiten the cashew nuts. Drain and boil the nuts in 1½ cups water with the turmeric. Add more water, if necessary, until the nuts are tender but not too soft.

Heat the ghee, brown the onions. Add in the green chilli, garlic, ginger, cloves, curry leaves and lemongrass. Stir in the coconut milk. Add salt, coriander powder and then the cashew nuts. Cook on a medium flame until almost dry. Stir with the handle of a wooden spoon to prevent breaking the cashew nuts.

Before serving add yoghurt and freshly chopped coriander and heat.

KATHAL KI SABZI
(RAW JACKFRUIT VEGETABLE)

SERVES: 6   PREPARATION TIME: 30 MINUTES

INGREDIENTS
Kathal (jackfruit)	1 kg, cut into 1½-inch pieces
Onions	2 large, grated
Tomato	1 large, grated
Adhrak-lahsun (ginger-garlic) paste	2 tbsp
Tejpatta (bay leaf)	2 leaves
Jeera (cumin) powder	½ tsp
Laal mirch (red chilli) powder	1 tsp

Haldi (turmeric) powder	1 tsp
Dhania (coriander) powder	1 tsp
Garam masala (ground spices)	2 tsp
Dahi (yoghurt)	4 tbsp
Mustard oil	2 cups, for frying
Hara dhania (fresh coriander)	12 leaves, finely chopped
Salt	1 tsp or to taste

METHOD

On your palms, rub a little mustard oil to prevent the jackfruit from sticking to your hands. Peel the jackfruit and cut into 1½-inch pieces. Keep the seeds of the jackfruit aside.

Heat the oil in a pan and deep-fry the jackfruit and seeds until they turn golden brown. Place on kitchen towels to absorb excess oil. In the same pan, add the bay leaves, grated onions, ginger and garlic paste and tomatoes with all the powdered masalas and salt and cook until they turn brown and the oil comes to the surface.

Next add the yoghurt and cook for 2 minutes so that the spices blend in with it. Add the fried jackfruit with ½ a cup of water and cook on a low flame for 10 minutes. Garnish with freshly chopped coriander leaves. Serve hot.

BHARWAAN TINDE
(STUFFED INDIAN SQUASH)

SERVES: 6   PREPARATION TIME: 30 MINUTES

INGREDIENTS

Tinda (Indian squash)	8 tender, medium, even-sized
Onions	3 medium, finely chopped
Hari mirch (green chilli)	4 medium, deseeded and finely chopped
Kalonji (black onion) seeds	1 tsp, coarsely ground
Jeera (cumin) seeds	1 tsp, coarsely ground
Methi (fenugreek) seeds	6 coarsely ground

Saunf (fennel) seeds	½ tsp, coarsely ground
Dhania (coriander) seeds	1 tsp, coarsely ground
Haldi (turmeric) powder	½ tsp
Laal mirch (red chilli)	1 tbsp, crushed
Limes	2 juiced
Oil	1 cup
Salt	1½ tsp or to taste

METHOD

Finely peel the tindas, cut off a thin slice from the top and remove the pulp. Keep aside the tops. Lightly steam the tindas in a double boiler and leave them to dry.

In a pan, sauté the onions in 2 tablespoons of oil, remove from the flame and add the coarsely ground spices. Let the mixture cool and then add the lemon juice.

Stuff the tindas with the onion and spice mixture. Securely cross-tie the tindas with their tops. On a low flame, heat the oil and fry the stuffed tindas. Then add the leftover spices and let the mixture cook. Serve hot.

DAHIWALE BAINGAN
(AUBERGINES/INDIAN EGGPLANT COOKED IN YOGHURT)

SERVES: 8–10   PREPARATION TIME: 40 MINUTES

INGREDIENTS

Baingan (aubergine, Indian eggplant)	3 large, sliced into rounds
Dahi (yoghurt)	2 cups
Lahsun (garlic) paste	½ tsp
Haldi (turmeric) powder	¼ tsp
Kaali sarson (black mustard) seeds	½ tsp
Sukhi laal mirch (dried red chillies)	2 whole, fried
Jeera (cumin) seeds	1 tsp, roasted and powdered
Laal mirch (red chilli) powder	½ tsp, for coating the baingan and ½ tsp for garnish
Lahsun (garlic)	6 cloves, fried for garnish

Sunflower oil	4 tbsp, for frying
Salt	1 tsp

METHOD

Sprinkle both sides of the baingan slices with turmeric, red chilli powder and salt. Heat the oil in a frying pan and then fry the baingan slices. Remove from the oil and put the baingan slices on paper towels to soak up the excess oil.

Gently beat the yoghurt and add to it the garlic paste, cumin powder, fried whole red chillies and the crispy fried garlic cloves. Pour the beaten yoghurt mixture into a large serving dish and place the golden fried aubergine slices on it.

Make a temper of fried mustard seeds, fried garlic and dried whole red chillies over the aubergines. Lightly sprinkle the red chilli powder and the aubergines are ready to be served.

Note: Instead of fried mustard seeds and red chillies, you can sprinkle two sprigs of chopped coriander leaves with a green chilli.

BHARWAAN BHINDI
(STUFFED OKRA)

SERVES: 8   PREPARATION TIME: 30 MINUTES

INGREDIENTS

Bhindi (okra)	750 gms, small, approximately 1½-inch each
Desi ghee	2 tbsp
Amchoor (dried mango) powder	1 tbsp
Dhania (coriander) powder	1 tbsp
Panch phoron masala	1½ tsp
Jeera (cumin) powder	1 tsp
Laal mirch (red chilli) powder	1 tsp
Haldi (turmeric) powder	1 tsp
Anaardana (pomegranate seed) powder	1 tbsp

Garam masala (ground spices)	1 tbsp
Sunflower oil	4 tbsp
Salt	1 tsp or to taste

METHOD

Wash the okra, spread it on paper towels and let it dry for 5–7 mins. Slice off the caps and tips of the okra and slit on one side.

Heat the oil, add the panch phoron masala. Separately in a small bowl add all the other ingredients together with water. Add this mixture to the panch phoron masala and roast it for 5 minutes. Let it cool.

Stuff this masala mixture inside the bhindi through the slit. Shallow-fry the bhindi in a frying pan, and cover it with a lid for 5 minutes, making sure that all the masalas soak in. Toss the bhindis, then cover and let them fry for 5 minutes. Serve hot.

KARELE KI SABZI
(SPICED BITTER GOURD)

SERVES: 8–10   PREPARATION TIME: 45 MINUTES

INGREDIENTS

Karela (bitter gourd)	½ kg, evenly-sized, not bigger than 2½ inches
Kairi (green mango)	3 tsp, ground to a paste
Dahi (yoghurt)	3 tbsp
Onions	3 medium, chopped
Hari mirch (green chilli)	4 pieces, whole
Dhania (coriander) powder	4 tsp
Haldi (turmeric) powder	2 tsp
Saunf (fennel) seeds	1 tsp
Kalonji (black onion) seeds	1 tsp
Gur (jaggery)	1 tsp
Mustard oil	3 tbsp
Salt	2 tsp

METHOD

Lightly scrape off the skins of the karelas, leaving most of it intact. Then slit the karelas from one side and scrape off the seeds. Sprinkle with salt and leave for 30 minutes. Slice them thinly into rounds.

Drop the karelas in boiling water for 3 minutes and remove. Let them cool. Remove from the water and squeeze out the excess water.

In the heated and smoked mustard oil, fry one-third of the chopped onion To this mixture, add the fennel seeds, black onion seeds, coriander powder, turmeric and the green mango paste. Add ½ a cup of water and then put in the boiled karelas, yoghurt, salt and the rest of the chopped onions and the whole green chillies.

Cook until the karelas are tender and the oil rises to the top. Just before taking the pan off the fire, sprinkle 1 teaspoon of powdered jaggery and mix it in to enhance the taste. Serve hot.

BHARWAAN SHIMLA MIRCH AUR MOTI HARI MIRCH
(STUFFED CAPSICUM AND STUFFED GREEN CHILLI)

SERVES: 8–10   PREPARATION TIME: 1 HOUR

INGREDIENTS

Aloo (potato)	250 gms, boiled
Kaala chana (black chickpeas)	100 gms, soaked for 2 hours and boiled
Hari mirch (green chilli)	500 gms, large
Shimla mirch (green capsicum)	8 small, with the stalk
Amchoor (dry mango) powder	1½ tsp
Garam masala (ground spices) powder	1 tsp
Dhania (coriander) powder	1 tsp
Haldi (turmeric) powder	1 tsp
Laal mirch (red chilli) powder	1 tsp
Anaardana (pomegranate seed) powder	1 tsp
Lime	2, juiced
Red chilli flakes	½ tsp
Oil	½ cup
Salt	2 tsp

METHOD

In a kadhai, add the coriander, turmeric, red chilli, garam masala and amchoor powders with 1 teaspoon salt. Sauté for 5 minutes in 2 tablespoons of oil. Add the boiled and mashed potatoes to this masala mixture and lightly brown, then remove from the flame and let it cool.

Add the red chilli flakes and 1 teaspoon salt to the boiled black chickpeas. Add this to the potato mixture. Squeeze the lime juice over the whole mixture and mix. Stuff this mixture inside the slit green chilli.

Cut off the caps of the capsicums and keep aside. Deseed the capsicums and stuff them generously with the aloo mixture, replace the caps on the capsicum and shallow-fry them in the remaining oil. The Bharwaan capsicums/chillies are ready to be served.

Option for the Bharwaan Chillies: Make a thin pakora mixture of 4 tablespoons of besan (chickpea flour), salt and ½ teaspoon of red chilli powder. Dip the stuffed chillies in this mixture and deep-fry them. Follow the same method as above.

BHARWAAN BAINGAN AUR DAHI KI PANEER
(AUBERGINE STUFFED WITH HUNG YOGHURT)

SERVES: 6–8   PREPARATION TIME: 30 MINUTES

INGREDIENTS

Aubergine	4 long, large
Sunflower oil	¾ cup
Ajwain (caraway) seeds	1½ tsp
Rock salt and black pepper	1 tsp each
Pomegranate	1 deseeded
Spice paste	1 tsp each of sesame seeds, red chilli flakes and caraway seeds

For the Stuffing:

Hung yoghurt	1½ cups
Sunflower oil	1½ tbsp
Garlic	4 cloves, crushed
Salt	to taste

METHOD

Pre-heat the oven to 200°C/400°F. Cut the aubergine into two halves, lengthwise, cutting straight through the green stalk (the stalk is for the look, not to be eaten). Use a small sharp knife to make three or four parallel and horizontal incisions in the cut side of each aubergine half, without cutting through to the skin.

Place the aubergine halves, cut side up, on a baking sheet lined with parchment paper. Brush them with oil. Keep brushing until all of the oil has been absorbed by the flesh. Sprinkle with the caraway seeds, salt and pepper. Roast for 35 to 40 minutes, at which point the flesh should be soft, flavourful and well browned. Remove from the oven and allow to cool down completely. While the aubergines are in the oven, cut the pomegranate and deseed the arils (seeds).

Whisk together all the ingredients and season the yoghurt with the spice paste. To serve, spoon plenty of lightly whisked yoghurt into the aubergine halves, without covering the stalks. Sprinkle a handful of pomegranate seeds on top of each aubergine half and serve.

SHAKARKANDI KA SALAD
(SWEET POTATO SALAD)

SERVES: 8   PREPARATION TIME: 10 MINUTES

INGREDIENTS

Shakarkandi (sweet potato)	1 kg	
Amrakh (carambola/star fruit)	4 medium, evenly sliced	
Chaat masala	2 tsp	
Lime juice	2 tbsp	
Salt	to taste	

METHOD

Roast the shakarkandi directly on a high flame. Once roasted, remove the skin and cut into 1-inch square pieces.

Put all the ingredients in a bowl and mix with chaat masala, salt and lime juice. Toss well. The salad is ready.

WHOLE GREEN PEAS WITH SESAME

SERVES: 8   PREPARATION TIME: 15 MINUTES

INGREDIENTS

Whole green peas	½ kg, fresh and tender
Dark sesame oil	2 tbsp
Black sesame seeds	4 tbsp

METHOD

Pick through the pea pods to remove any that are not perfect. Remove the stem end and the string from each pod. Lightly baste the peas with oil and toss them on a heated pan over a low flame.

In a bowl, sprinkle the peas with sesame seeds and dark sesame oil for the flavour. Serve at room temperature.

VEGETABLE CUTLETS

This was an Anglo-Indian speciality, found in all railway station dining rooms, now defunct.

SERVES: 8   PREPARATION TIME: 1 HOUR

INGREDIENTS

Peas	50 gms
French beans	50 gms
Potatoes	5 medium, boiled and peeled
Onion	1 medium, finely chopped
Sitaphal (ripened pumpkin)*	50 gms, boiled and mashed
Carrot	50 gms, grated
Maida (refined flour)	1 cup
Garam masala (ground spices)	1 tsp
Kaali mirch (black pepper)	1 tsp
Sunflower oil	4 tbsp
Salt	1 tsp

*In Uttar Pradesh, custard apple is called sharifa and pumpkin is called sitaphal.

METHOD

Boil the potatoes and the pumpkin separately. Then peel the potatoes and the pumpkin, cut into small pieces and mash them together. Finely chop all the remaining vegetables and add these to the mashed pumpkin and potatoes. Wet your palms and form the cutlet-shaped patties.

Spread the flour on a large flat plate, flip these patties in the flour until evenly covered. Heat the oil in a frying pan. Reduce the flame and add the cutlets one by one. Fry until golden brown, then flip the cutlet to the other side until that too is golden brown and remove. The cutlets are ready to be served hot.

CARROT SOUFFLÉ

SERVES: 8   PREPARATION TIME: 20 MINUTES

INGREDIENTS

Mayonnaise	1½ cup (see page 219)	
Carrots	1 cup, grated	
Eggs	2 egg whites	
Gelatin powder	2 tbsp	
Nutmeg	¼ tsp	

For garnishing:

Capsicum	1 small, scraped out and cut into fine round slices
Green olives	6 whole without stones, cut into small rounds
Egg	1 hard-boiled and sliced

METHOD

Mix the gelatin in ½ a cup of cold water, warm in a bain-marie or double boiler until it dissolves completely. Then mix the carrot, mayonnaise and nutmeg in a mixer for 1 minute. Slowly add the gelatin using the mixer only for short bursts of a few seconds. Transfer to a glass bowl.

Beat the egg whites until they are stiff and slowly fold into the carrot mixture. Cover and refrigerate for 2 hours.

Overturn the soufflé onto a flat serving dish and decorate it with roundels of the egg, capsicum and olives. The soufflé is ready to be served. If the soufflé is not served immediately, it should be kept refrigerated.

Mutton with Vegetables

For Muslims, adding meat to any kind of vegetable was a common way of cooking. Soon all non-vegetarian Hindu families followed suit. The best examples are Palak Gosht and Shalgam Gosht, which are our house specialities. In these the flavours of the vegetables are enhanced once they are cooked with the meat to which several aromatic spices have been added. Dopiaza, a Persian word for two onions, was a Middle Eastern dish from Afghan cuisine where the onions were added in two stages. Kairi ka Do Pyaza evolved in Lucknow from this Afghani dish and became a seasonal speciality. According to legend, the dish was created when a courtier of the Mughal empire from Afghanistan, Akbar Mullah Do Piaza, accidentally added a large quantity of onions to a mutton dish.

While full bitter gourd (karelas) could be stuffed with potatoes and other masala combinations, Bharwaan Keema Karelas were typically Lucknowi. Similarly, Jeera Aloo ka Gosht was a speciality of the Kayastha community of Lucknow.

My mother's Irish Stew is a great favourite. It is nutritious and a substantial meal on its own. Our guests and family wholeheartedly savoured this stew which has always been considered among the best in the city. For the family, particularly during the winter months, it has been our dinner time comfort food.

KAIRI KA DO PYAZA
(MUTTON/CHICKEN COOKED WITH RAW MANGOES AND ONIONS)

SERVES: 8   PREPARATION TIME: 1 HOUR

INGREDIENTS

Mutton	750 gms
Or	
Chicken	1 kg, cut into 12 pieces
Onions	12 medium, thickly sliced
Kairi (raw mango)	4 peeled, cut thinly lengthwise
Hari mirch (green chilli)	8 whole and deseeded
Adhrak-lahsun (ginger-garlic) paste	1 tbsp each
Laal mirch (red chilli) powder	1 tbsp
Haldi (turmeric) powder	1 tsp
Karhi patta (curry leaves)	12 small leaves
Salt	2 tsp or to taste
Sunflower oil	1 cup

METHOD

Combine all the ingredients, except the raw mangoes, in a saucepan and cook on a low flame. Do not add any water, as the liquid from the onions will be enough to cook the meat. Stir frequently.

When the liquid reduces, cook the meat on a high flame until it becomes tender, stir again, then add the raw mango slices and cook for 10 minutes. Serve hot.

BHARWAAN KEEMA KARELA
(STUFFED BITTER GOURD)

SERVES: 8   PREPARATION TIME: 1 HOUR

INGREDIENTS

Minced mutton	½ kg
Karela (bitter gourd)	12 pieces

Onion	1 large, finely sliced
Adhrak-lahsun (ginger-garlic) paste	2 tbsp
Imli (tamarind)	1 tsp, thick juice
Hari mirch (green chilli)	3–4 pieces, deseeded and finely chopped
Laal mirch (red chilli) powder	1 tsp
Haldi (turmeric) powder	1 tsp
Saunf (fennel seeds)	½ tsp
Kalonji (onion) seeds	½ tbsp
Gur (jaggery)	2 tbsp
Sunflower oil	½ cup
Salt	1 tsp or to taste

METHOD

Thouroughly wash the karelas, then coarsely scrape with a sharp knife. Cut each karela lengthwise and remove the seeds. Do not wash again. Mix together the salt, turmeric and 1 tablespoon of jaggery, rub this mixture onto the karelas and leave for half an hour. Then wash them well under cold water and let them drain in a colander.

Heat the oil in a pan and fry the onions until they are golden brown. Remove and set aside. In the same pan put the minced mutton with all the ingredients except the jaggery, green chillies and tamarind. When the liquid has been absorbed, add the fried onions and green chillies and cover the pan. Cook on a low flame for 5 minutes. Remove from the flame and let the mince cool down.

Stuff the karelas with the minced meat masala and tie them with a thick thread. Heat the remaining oil and shallow-fry the karelas in a non-stick frying pan until they turn golden brown. Then add the tamarind juice with the remaining jaggery and cook on a low flame for 15 minutes or until the oil rises to the surface. Serve the karelas individually laid out on a flat serving dish.

PALAK GOSHT
(MUTTON WITH SPINACH)

SERVES: 8   PREPARATION TIME: 1½ HOURS

INGREDIENTS

Palak (spinach)	1 kg, washed and chopped
Mutton (gol boti)	750 gms from the leg, cut into 2-inch pieces, with the bone
Onions	2 medium, peeled and finely chopped
Tomatoes	2 large, grated with the peels removed
Dahi (yoghurt)	50 gms
Lahsun (garlic)	8 cloves, peeled
Adhrak (ginger) paste	1 tsp
Lahsun (garlic) paste	1 tbsp
Garam masala (ground spices)	4 tsp
Meat masala	1 tbsp
Haldi (turmeric) powder	1 tsp
Laal mirch (red chilli)	½ tsp, ground
Tejpatta (bay leaf)	2 leaves
Badi elaichi (black cardamom)	3 pods
Dalchini (cinnamon)	2-inch piece
Desi ghee	4 tbsp
Salt	1 tsp or to taste

METHOD

Heat the desi ghee, add the bay leaf, black cardamom and cinnamon. Then add the finely chopped onions, brown them and add the ginger and garlic paste along with the grated tomatoes. Add all the masalas together and let the mixture cook for 5 minutes. Then add the yoghurt and cook for a further 5 minutes. Add the meat and brown it well for 40 minutes, until it is well cooked.

In a heavy-bottomed pan of boiling water, boil the spinach for 1 minute, to retain the colour and remove the dirt. Remove from the flame, put it in a colander under cold water and squeeze out all the water and coarsely chop the spinach. Add the spinach to the meat curry and cook for 5 minutes until the spinach coats the meat well. Serve hot.

ALOO GOSHT KA SAALAN
(MUTTON CURRY WITH POTATOES)

SERVES: 8   PREPARATION TIME: 1 HOUR

INGREDIENTS

Mutton (gol boti)	750 gms, from the leg, cut into 2-inch pieces with the bone
Aloo (potato)	6 medium, quartered
Onions	250 gms, chopped
Tomatoes	250 gms, finely chopped
Adhrak (ginger)	1-inch piece, chopped
Lahsun (garlic)	6 cloves, chopped
Jeera (cumin) seeds	½ tsp, freshly roasted
Tejpatta (bay leaf)	2 leaves
Badi elaichi (black cardamom)	2 pods
Hari elaichi (green cardamom)	4 pods
Dalchini (cinnamon) stick	2-inch piece
Laung (cloves)	4 cloves
Javitri (mace)	½ an inch
Jeera (cumin) powder	1 tsp
Garam masala (ground spices) powder	1 tsp
Dhania (coriander) powder	2 tsp
Laal mirch (red chilli) powder	1 tsp
Sunflower oil	½ cup
Salt	1 tbsp or to taste

METHOD

Heat the oil and add the roasted cumin seeds. Prick the potatoes with a fork and fry until they turn a golden brown. Remove the potatoes and set aside. Remove the pan from the flame and strain the oil to separate the cumin seeds.

Reheat the oil and fry the onions until they turn golden brown. Add all the whole spices and continue to fry until the onions are browned. Then add all the powdered spices and stir for 5 minutes. Add the chopped ginger and garlic and fry for another minute.

Add ½ a cup of water to the mutton and cook for 10 minutes.

Then add the tomatoes and let the meat cook in it until the water from the tomatoes reduces. Then add 3 cups of water and salt. Cover and cook the meat over a medium flame for about 40 minutes, until it becomes tender. Finally, add the fried potatoes and cook for 5 minutes, gently mixing them in with the tender meat. Serve hot.

SHALGAM GOSHT
(MUTTON WITH TURNIPS)

SERVES: 8   PREPARATION TIME: 1½ HOURS

INGREDIENTS

Shalgam (turnips)	½ kg, large, quartered
Mutton (gol boti)	750 gms, from the leg, cut into 2-inch pieces with the bone marrow
Onions	2 medium, peeled and finely chopped
Tomatoes	2 large, grated with the peels removed
Dahi (yoghurt)	¼ cup
Lahsun (garlic) cloves	8 cloves, chopped
Adhrak (ginger) paste	1 tsp
Lahsun (garlic) paste	1 tbsp
Garam masala (ground spices)	4 tsp
Laal mirch (red chilli)	½ tsp, ground
Haldi (turmeric) powder	1 tsp
Meat masala	1 tbsp
Tejpatta (bay leaf)	2 leaves
Badi elaichi (black cardamom)	3 pods
Dalchini (cinnamon)	2-inch piece
Desi ghee	4 tbsp
Salt	1 tbsp or to taste

METHOD
Heat the desi ghee, add the bay leaves, black cardamom and cinnamon. Then add the finely chopped onions, brown them and add the ginger and garlic pastes along with the grated tomatoes.

Add all the masalas and the salt together, let the mixture cook for

5 minutes and then add the yoghurt. Cook again for 5 minutes. Then add the meat and brown it for 40 minutes, until it is well cooked.

To this meat curry, add the pieces of turnip and roast them well with the curry. Add 2 cups of water for the gravy, let it come to a boil and then cover it with a lid for 10 minutes. Serve hot and garnished with coarsely chopped fresh coriander leaves.

IRISH STEW

SERVES: 8   PREPARATION TIME: 1 HOUR

INGREDIENTS

Shoulder of mutton	500 gms, cut into 3-inch pieces with the bones
Onion	1 large, cut into 4 pieces
Aloo (potato)	1 peeled and cut into 6 pieces
Gajar (carrots)	4 peeled and cut into thick long strips
Phool gobi (cauliflower)	1 broken into florets
Adhrak (ginger)	1-inch piece, julienned
Hari mirch (green chilli)	4 whole with stalks
Baby potatoes	10 small and peeled
Baby onions	10 small and peeled
Badi elaichi (black cardamom)	2 pods
Dalchini (cinnamon)	2 sticks of ½-inch each
Laung (cloves)	4–6 cloves
Kaali mirch (black peppercorn)	10 peppercorns
Refined oil	1 tbsp
Salt	1 tbsp or to taste

For the white Sauce:

Refined oil	1 tsp
Maida (refined flour)	2 tbsp
Milk	2 cups, warmed
Double cream (optional)	1 tbsp, beaten

METHOD

Heat the oil in a pressure cooker and sauté the cardamom, cinnamon, cloves and black peppercorns for a minute. Add the meat and sauté on a high flame so that the juices of the meat get sealed. If required, keep sprinkling water on the meat so that it does not burn. Sauté for about 5 more minutes.

Add the onion, potato and ginger. Stir and mix for a minute. Add salt and enough hot water so that some gravy will be left after the meat has been cooked.

Pressure cook for 20 minutes, first on a high flame, then lower the flame and cook until the meat is tender. Let the steam go down on its own. Open the pressure cooker and check whether the meat is three-fourths cooked. If so, add the baby potatoes and the baby onions. After 5 minutes, add the carrots, cauliflower and whole green chillies and cook for another 5 minutes.

To make the white sauce, heat the oil in a pan. Add the flour and when it starts bubbling, remove from the flame and add warm milk. Gradually beat the mixture thoroughly, so that there are no lumps. Cook the sauce until it thickens and add to the stew. Let the stew simmer for about 10 minutes, being careful that the vegetables are not overcooked.

Add the beaten cream, mix well and remove the pan from the heat. When serving, remove the green chillies and whole spices. Serve with toasted bread or boiled rice.

Mutton

Lucknow has always specialized in meat recipes, some of which are simple and some are more complex. Keema is an old Turkish word for minced or pounded meat. It was an easy and effortless way of cooking meat to make it tender. The Mughals liked minced beef, whereas in Lucknow goat meat was preferred. The tastiest kind of keema preparations were made by the trusted nanbais (bazaar cooks) of Lucknow, who specialized in one particular dish.

A famous speciality of Lucknow is Kairi Keema, made with raw green mangoes which gives the minced meat a delicious hint of fruit with a tart flavour. This is a great favourite at the home of our friend Jimmy Jahangirabad, where it is cooked to perfection.

My father used to say, 'You can discern a good cook from the way he prepares a korma.' He was right. There is absolutely no better curry than a well-cooked korma. The word korma was probably derived from the Persian word koresh, which was a mild stew made with ghee. This was Indianized by the Mughals when they started adding yoghurt, cream, ground almonds and fragrant spices to it. The most popular of the korma curries of Lucknow is Shahi Korma, which is similar to the traditional korma recipe but is laced with heavy cream. Many households make wonderful kormas and one of the best is in the home of our close friend Wajahat Habibullah and his family.

Shabhdeg, a seasonal yet delicious dish, probably of Kashmiri origin, is a complex combination of boneless chunks of meat, koftas and turnips (shalgam). Shabh means night and deg means a large cooking pot. This unique dish is prepared overnight, on a simmering flame. The best shabhdeg in all of Awadh is cooked in the kitchens of Jahangirabad Palace. We have fond memories of overindulging ourselves there, during the season of cooking shabhdeg.

Khubani ka Saalan (Apricot Curry) is a house speciality. This again is a seasonal dish, made when fresh apricots are available. The original recipe travelled all the way from Afghanistan—where apricots grew profusely—to Lahore and then was introduced to Lucknow, via Sher Shah Sur's famous Grand Trunk Road.

Lahori Bhuna Gosht was introduced to Lucknow by my mother along with the most delicious Bhunay Mutton Chops. Both these recipes are easy to cook and hard to resist.

The recipe for Nargisi Koftas, with their history and their fine distinction from Qudums, another form of these koftas, was given to me by my school friend, Parveen Talha. The recipe for Khichhra, which is traditionally made by Shia families during Muharram, is from Zakia Zaheer who is a great cook and a Persian scholar.

KAIRI KEEMA
(RAW MANGOES WITH MINCED MUTTON)

SERVES: 6   PREPARATION TIME: 40 MINUTES

INGREDIENTS

Mutton (minced)	½ kg lean meat from the leg
Kairi (raw mango)	3 finely chopped
Onions	3 medium, finely chopped
Pudina (mint) leaves	1 bunch, finely chopped
Dhania (coriander) leaves	1 bunch, finely chopped
Hari mirch (green chilli)	4 finely chopped
Adhrak (ginger)	1 tbsp, finely chopped
Adhrak-lahsun (ginger-garlic) paste	1 tbsp
Laal mirch (red chilli) powder	½ tbsp
Haldi (turmeric) powder	1 tsp
Karhi patta (curry leaf)	7–8 small leaves
Kalonji (onion) seeds	½ tsp
Oil	½ cup
Salt	1 tsp or to taste

METHOD

Combine the minced meat, ginger and garlic paste, red chilli powder, turmeric and salt in a pan. Cook on a low flame until the liquid from the mince reduces.

In the same pan, to the oil add the raw mangoes, onions, chopped ginger, onion seeds, green chilli and curry leaves and cook, stirring frequently for about 10 minutes. Add the chopped mint and the coriander leaves. Cover and let it simmer on a low flame for 5 minutes. Serve hot.

RAAN MUSSALAM
(ROASTED LEG OF GOAT)

SERVES: 8   PREPARATION TIME: 2 HOURS

INGREDIENTS

Mutton	1 kg, lean leg piece, well washed and cleaned
Kaccha papita (raw papaya)	½ cup, crushed

For the Marinade:

Dahi (yoghurt)	1 cup
Besan (gram flour)	1 tbsp, roasted
Onions	200 gms, sliced, fried until golden brown then ground to a paste
Adhrak (ginger) paste	3 tsp
Lahsun (garlic) paste	3 tsp
Laal mirch (red chilli) powder	2 tsp
Kesar (saffron)	6 strands
Yellow colour	3–4 drops
Ghee	1½ cups
Salt	1 tbsp

For the Stuffing:

Kaju (cashew nuts)	1½ cups, lightly roasted
Kalonji (onion) seeds	5 tsp, lightly roasted
Khus-khus (poppy) seeds	4 tbsp, well washed, dried and lightly roasted
Sukha nariyal (dry coconut)	1 tbsp, grated
Hari elaichi (green cardamom)	4 pods
Badi elaichi (black cardamom)	2 pods
Kaali mirch (black peppercorns)	12 peppercorns
Laung (cloves)	6 cloves
Jaiphal (nutmeg)	1½ pieces
Javitri (mace)	2 pieces

For the Garnish:

Badaam (almonds)	10 finely chopped
Chandi ka varq (silver leaves)	2 leaves

METHOD

Generously smear the leg of the mutton with raw papaya, rubbing it in so that the mutton soaks in the juice. Marinate for 2 hours.

Grind the cashew nuts, onion seeds and poppy seeds along with the grated coconut to a paste. Separately, grind the green and black cardamoms, the peppercorns, the cloves, the nutmeg and the mace. Mix these in with the cashew paste.

Mix the yoghurt, red chilli powder, onion paste, ginger and garlic pastes, saffron and the yellow colour along with the gram flour and salt. Apply this marinade evenly on the leg of mutton and let it marinate for 2 hours.

Place a lagan* on a medium flame. Pour in the ghee and put the mutton leg in the pot along with the marinade. Cover with its lid and put 2–3 burning charcoals in a metal bowl on top of it. Dum cook for 15–20 minutes. Remove the lid and turn the leg over, again cover and dum cook for 15 minutes until the meat becomes tender.

Remove the meat leg from the lagan and place on a large roast dish, garnish with the silver leaves and chopped almonds. Serve hot.

KHUBANI KA SAALAN
(DRIED APRICOTS AND MEAT CURRY)

Khubani or dried apricots add a wonderful sweet-and-sour flavour to this exotic meat preparation. The origin of this dish can be traced to Kandahar in Afghanistan. Awadhi cuisine is an amalgamation of Persian, Afghani and Arabic cuisines that mutated into a distinct Lucknow cuisine…all part of the foods and culture that travelled down the Silk Road from Constantinople.

---

*A lagan is a wide and heavy-bottomed utensil with a tight lid, often used in Lucknowi cooking.

INGREDIENTS

Mutton*	1 kg, lean leg of mutton, chopped into 2½-inch pieces
Dried apricots	300 gms, soaked in water
Onions	500 gms, finely chopped
Adhrak-lahsun (ginger-garlic) paste	2 tsp, levelled
Tejpatta (bay leaf)	2 leaves
Javitri (mace)	1 piece
Dalchini (cinnamon)	1-inch stick
Hari elaichi (green cardamoms)	6 pods
Laung (cloves)	6 cloves
Dhania (coriander) powder	2 tbsp
Haldi (turmeric) powder	1 tbsp
Laal mirch (red chilli) powder	1 tsp, heaped
Kashmiri laal mirch (red chilli) powder	3 tsp
Saunf (fennel) powder	1 tsp
Dhania (coriander) leaves	½ cup, finely chopped
Garam masala (ground spices) powder	to taste
Oil	¾ cup
Salt	to taste

METHOD

Heat the oil in a heavy-bottomed pan. Add the bay leaves, cardamoms, cloves, cinnamon and mace flower and fry until the spices start to sputter.

Add the finely chopped onions to the tempered oil and fry them until they turn golden brown. Add the coriander powder, turmeric, red chilli powder, salt and Kashmiri chilli powder to the pan and cook for 30 seconds. Add the ginger and garlic paste and the meat to the pan, sauté for 10–15 minutes. Add enough water to cook the meat until it is half-done.

Add the dried apricots to the gravy and cover the pan with a lid and cook on a low flame until the meat is tender and succulent. Add the garam masala powder and the fennel seed powder. Cook

*Lean leg of mutton from a small goat, ideally the bone should have marrow.

for another 5 minutes until the oil rises to the top of the gravy. The prepared gravy should be thick and blended well.

Remove the bay leaves, cinnamon and mace, if intact, before serving. Garnish with freshly chopped coriander leaves.

LAHORI BHUNA GOSHT
(ROASTED MUTTON)

SERVES: 8   PREPARATION TIME: 1½ HOURS

INGREDIENTS

Mutton	1 kg, lean leg of mutton, chopped into 2½-inch pieces
Dahi (yoghurt)	½ cup
Onions	2 medium, chopped
Adhrak (ginger)	2 tbsp, finely chopped
Lahsun (garlic)	1 tbsp, finely chopped
Hara dhania (coriander)	1½ tbsp, finely chopped
Hari mirch (green chillies)	4 finely chopped with the seeds
Kaali mirch (black peppercorn)	1 tsp, ground
Badi elaichi (black cardamom)	1 tsp
Flour	1 tbsp
Lime juice	1 tbsp
Vegetable oil	2 tbsp
Salt	1 tsp or to taste

METHOD

Wash the meat well and place it in a bowl. Add the ginger, garlic, green chillies, coriander, lemon juice, peppercorns, salt, oil and yoghurt and mix them well with the mutton. Marinate it in the fridge for 2 hours.

Heat the oil in a pressure cooker and add the mutton with the marinade, black cardamoms and onions and brown the mutton. Add enough water for it to cook in a pressure cooker for 20 minutes. Allow it to cool.

Remove the pressure cooker lid, cover the cooker with an ordinary lid and simmer the roast for another 15 minutes or until the mutton is tender and the liquid has reduced. Remove the mutton and keep aside. Strain the stock.

In another pan, add a little flour and sauté until it is light golden. Add one cup of the mutton stock and cook on a low flame until it is slightly thick. Pour this mutton stock over the roasted mutton and on a low flame allow the stock to seep into the mutton. Serve hot.

SHAHI KORMA
(SAFFRON-FLAVOURED RICH MUTTON GRAVY)

SERVES: 8   PREPARATION TIME: 1½ HOURS

INGREDIENTS

Mutton	1kg, gol boti
Yoghurt (dahi)	4 tbsp
Onions	5 medium, finely sliced
Adhrak (ginger) paste	2 tbsp
Lahsun (garlic) paste	2 tbsp
Khus-khus (poppy) seeds	1 tsp, washed and ground to a paste
Hari elaichi (green cardamom)	5 pods
Badi elaichi (black cardamom)	2 pods
Laung (cloves)	5 cloves
Dalchini (cinnamon)	2 sticks
Tejpatta (bay leaf)	2 leaves
Javitri (mace)	2 pieces
Dhania (coriander) powder	2 tsp
Laal mirch (red chilli) powder	1 tsp
Garam masala (ground spices)	1½ tsp
Safed mirch (white pepper) powder	1 tsp
Kewra (screw pine) water	2 drops
Kesar (saffron)	12–14 strands, dissolved in 2 tbsp warmed milk
Ghee	4 tbsp
Water	1½ cups

Badaam (almonds)	20 blanched, skinned
Onion rings	2 small onions, fried for garnish
Salt	1 tbsp or to taste

METHOD

Marinate the mutton in yoghurt and keep aside for an hour. Heat the ghee in a heavy-bottomed pan. Add the finely sliced onions and lightly fry them until they are golden brown. Remove from the flame and set the pan aside.

In a pot, add the ginger and garlic pastes, cloves, coriander powder, red chilli powder, green cardamoms, black cardamom, cinnamon, bay leaf, mace and poppy seeds and stir for a few minutes. Add the mutton, water and salt, mix well. Cover the pot and cook on a low flame for about 30 minutes. Then add the browned onions to the mutton and stir again.

Cover and cook for an hour, or until the mutton is tender. Then add the screwpine water, white pepper and ground spices masala. Add the saffron liquid to the mutton gravy to enhance the flavour and the aroma. Garnish the mutton with thin deep-fried onion rings and blanched almond halves. Serve hot.

SHABHDEG
(MUTTON COOKED WITH TURNIPS)

SERVES: 8   PREPARATION TIME: 1 HOUR AND OVERNIGHT

INGREDIENTS

Mutton	1 kg, cut into small pieces
Keema (minced meat)	½ kg
Shalgam (turnips)	250 gms, medium and even-sized
Onions	5 medium, finely chopped
Dahi (yoghurt)	2 cups, beaten
Malai (heavy cream)	250 gms, beaten
Badaam (almond) paste	50 gms
Lahsun (garlic) paste	3 tbsp

Adhrak (ginger) paste	3 tbsp
Kaccha papita (raw papaya) paste	2 tbsp
Laung (cloves)	5 cloves
Dalchini (cinnamon)	2 sticks
Hari elaichi (green cardamom)	3 pods
Haldi (turmeric) powder	1½ tsp
Garam masala (ground spices)	2 tsp
Jeera (cumin) powder	2½ tsp
Shahi jeera (black cumin) powder	1½ tsp, fried
Laal mirch (red chilli) powder	1½ tbsp
Lemon juice	2 tbsp
Kesar (saffron)	2 tbsp, dissolved in warm milk
Kewra (screw pine) water	2 drops
Ghee	2 cups
Salt	to taste

METHOD

Roast the turnips on a tawa. Remove and peel the skins. Prick lightly with a fork. Rub half the garlic paste, turmeric and salt on the turnips and put them aside for 15–20 minutes.

Heat the ghee in a saucepan. Fry the turnips until they turn golden brown. Remove and keep aside. In the same ghee fry the onions until they are crisp and golden brown.

Meanwhile, grind the cinnamon, cloves and the green cardamoms to a paste.

To prepare the yakhni (soup), put half of the fried onions in a saucepan along with half of the ginger and garlic pastes, half of the clove, cardamom and cinnamon pastes, half of the mutton pieces and enough water to cook the meat to a very soft texture so that it can be strained to obtain a yakhni. When the meat is done, remove the bones and mash the pulp. Then strain it through a sieve or a muslin cloth. The yakhni is ready. Keep aside.

Then mix the minced meat, the papaya paste and the remaining ginger and garlic paste, the cloves and the cinnamon-green cardamom paste with ½ teaspoon of garam masala powder. Keep aside for 30 minutes.

Shape the minced meat into koftas or balls, approximately the same size as the turnips. Deep-fry and keep aside.

In the remaining ghee, add the remainder of the mutton pieces, cumin, the fried black cumin, red chilli powder and garam masala powder and fry until the meat turns brown. Add the yakhni, yoghurt, beaten cream, almond paste, fried turnips, lamb koftas and the lime juice. Stir gently. Add sufficient water for a thick gravy and to cook the meat. Add the remaining garam masala and salt.

Cover the pot with a tight lid and seal the edges with kneaded dough. Dum cook by placing burning charcoal in a metal bowl on the lid. Let it simmer through the night. When the pot is opened, the ghee should have risen to the surface. Mix in the saffron mixture. Serve hot.

BHUNAY MUTTON CHOPS

SERVES: 8   PREPARATION TIME: 1 HOUR

INGREDIENTS

Mutton	1 kg, single chops from the breast
Onions	3 medium, finely chopped
Tomatoes	3 medium, finely chopped
Adhrak (ginger) paste	1 tbsp
Lahsun (garlic) paste	1 tbsp
Dalchini (cinnamon)	1 stick
Tejpatta (bay leaf)	2 leaves
Laung (cloves)	10 cloves
Badi elaichi (black cardamom)	2 pods
Garam masala (ground spices)	1 tbsp
Meat masala	1 tbsp
Dhania (coriander) powder	1 tbsp
Laal mirch (red chilli) powder	1 tsp
Kaali mirch (peppercorns)	6 peppercorns
Dahi (yoghurt)	1 cup
Desi ghee	6 tbsp
Salt	2 tsp

METHOD

Wash and dry the mutton chops. Keep aside.

In a kadhai, melt the ghee and add the bay leaves and the finely chopped onions and fry them until they turn golden brown. Then add the ginger and garlic pastes, tomatoes and all the powdered masalas and spices.

Next, add the yoghurt and then the mutton chops. Cook on a medium flame for 15 minutes, until the meat turns golden brown. Add ½ a cup of water and cook for another 15 minutes on a low flame, tossing occasionally. Serve hot.

NARGISI KOFTA
(MINCED MEAT STUFFED WITH EGGS)

SERVES: 4   PREPARATION TIME: 1 HOUR

INGREDIENTS

Mutton	250 gms, minced
Eggs	4 hard-boiled and shelled
Onion	1 small, finely chopped
Onion	1 thinly sliced
Onion paste	1 tbsp
Lahsun (garlic paste)	2 tsp
Adhrak (ginger paste)	2 tsp
Dahi (yoghurt)	1¼ cup
Chana ka atta (Bengal gram flour)	2 tbsp
Khus-khus (poppy) seeds	1 tsp, well washed, ground to a paste
Badi elaichi (black cardamom)	4 pods
Laung (cloves)	3 cloves
Kaali mirch (black peppercorns)	5 peppercorns
Jeera (cumin) seeds	½ tsp
Laal mirch (red chilli) powder	1 tsp
Salt	to taste
Oil	½ cup

METHOD

Over a medium flame, heat the oil in a pan and fry the chopped onions to a golden brown colour. Remove from the oil and keep aside to let the onions cool. Grind the onions to a paste with the yoghurt and keep aside.

Mix half of the onion paste and half of the ginger and garlic pastes with salt. Then add the onion mixture and gram flour to the minced mutton and mix it well. Divide this mixture into four equal portions, and form each portion into a patty, then place a hard-boiled egg in the centre of each patty and gently wrap the meat around all four eggs. On a high flame, in a kadhai, deep-fry each egg and set it aside.

For the curry, heat the oil in a pan and add the remaining fried onion paste with the sliced onions, ginger and garlic paste, red chilli powder, poppy seed paste and salt. Also add all the whole spices and fry them well, until the oil rises to the surface. Then add the yoghurt mixture and mix it in well. Remove from the flame.

Halve the fried boiled eggs lengthwise and place them in the curry on a flat platter. Serve hot.

Note: When the egg koftas are cut across, they are called Nargisi Koftas; when cut lengthwise they are called Qudums.

KHICHHRA

INGREDIENTS

Mutton or chicken	1 kg, boneless
Chana lentil	250 gms, soaked for 1½ hours
Moong lentil	125 gms, soaked for 1½ hours
Masoor lentil	125 gms, soaked for 1½ hours
Urad lentil	125 gms, soaked for 1½ hours
Wheat dalia (coarsely powdered whole wheat)	½ kg, soaked for 1 hour
Rice	125 gms, soaked
Garam masala (ground spices)	1 tbsp
Soda bicarbonate	1 tsp

For the meat:

Adhrak-lahsun (ginger-garlic) paste	2 tbsp
Dahi (yoghurt)	250 gms
Laal mirch (red chilli)	1½ tbsp, powdered
Dhania (coriander)	2 tbsp, powdered
Garam masala (ground spices)	½ tbsp
Haldi (turmeric) powder	1 tsp
Oil	1½ cup
Salt	to taste

Accompaniments:

Pudina (mint)	1 bunch, finely chopped
Dhania (fresh coriander)	1 bunch, finely chopped
Hari mirch (green chillies)	10 finely chopped
Limes	6, cut into eight pieces
Jeera (cumin seeds)	2 tbsp, roasted and powdered
Salt	to taste

For Baghar (tempering):

Onion	4 medium, finely sliced
Desi ghee	1½ cups

METHOD

In a pan, add the wheat dalia along with 2–3 glasses of water and 2 tablespoons of oil. Cook on a low flame. When the wheat starts to soften add 1 teaspoon of soda bicarbonate. Cook until it becomes tender.

Wash all the soaked lentils in warm water. Cook on a low flame until the lentils are tender. Drain, cool and then grind them.

Boil the rice until it becomes very soft and keep it aside. In a large pot combine the meat, all the spices and oil and cook on medium flame stirring frequently. When the liquid from the meat is absorbed, add the softened wheat dalia with a cup of water, stir and cook until the meat becomes tender and mixes with the wheat dalia.

Then add the lentils with the rice along with a little water and continue to stir. Put a tawa on a high flame and place the pot on it. If the khichhra seems too thick add two more glasses of water and leave on a very low flame, stirring frequently. When all the ingredients have combined completely the khichhra is ready.

Make a baghar (temper) by frying the onions in desi ghee until they become golden brown. Pour some over the khichhra and keep the remaining onions aside to serve as an accompaniment along with the freshly chopped mint and coriander leaves, green chillies, limes, fried onions and roasted cumin seeds along with the ghee used for frying the onions to pour over the khichhra. Serve hot.

Chicken

A great chicken recipe which has been passed on to me by my mother is Dahi Chicken. This preparation is quite different from other yoghurt-based chicken recipes. This original recipe of my mother's is always appreciated by everyone. When I learnt it, I added a few of my own inputs to this recipe. My mother approves! This recipe has also been taught to my mother's granddaughters and her great-grandchildren. In my mother's home, cooking is an idea and an experiment which has often resulted in a new culinary invention.

One of the lesser-known recipes from the royal kitchens of Lucknow is Murgh Wajid Ali, named after the last nawab of Awadh, Wajid Ali Shah. He was a great patron of the arts and was deeply interested in all forms of culture, of which fine cuisine was an integral part. He was famous for his royal kitchens and the culinary skills of his many cooks, who competed with each other to prepare the most unusual delicacies.

Another well-known lavish preparation from Lucknow is Murgh-e-Mussalam, where the whole chicken is marinated and prepared with exotic spices, stuffed with eggs and generously decorated with almonds and silver leaves (chandi ka varq). Murgh-e-Mussalam in *Ain-i-Akbari* (The Constitution of Akbar) is referred to as Musamman. This later evolved into Murgh-e-Mussalam, described by Ibn Battuta, the fourteenth-century scholar and traveller, as one of the most favoured dishes at the court of Sultan Muhammad bin Tughlaq. Another variation of this is Raan Mussalam. In this a leg of lamb is marinated overnight and cooked on a slow fire. For Machhli Mussalam, whole fish fillets are marinated in yoghurt and spices.

My brother and sister-in-law, Ashok and Shuchi Sur, are good hosts and great cooks. Everyone in the family has a few signature dishes that they prepare superbly. Ashok learnt Murgh-e-Mussalam from their good friend Kaneez Nargis Raza, fondly known as Nabaat. Ashok enjoys cooking this mussalam when he entertains his close friends. For years, it has been his signature dish. Some of my mother's angrezi khana recipes are Chicken Roast in Yoghurt, Chicken à la Scala and Chicken Chasseur. Our khansama (cook) found it very difficult to pronounce the name of the latter dish. He always referred to Chicken Chasseur as Firangi Chicken Curry.

Murgh Zaffrani and Dhania Murgh ka Korma are both delicate recipes. They are essentially a hallmark of Lucknowi cuisine. One has the colour and aroma of saffron and the other is full of the fresh flavours of green coriander.

Kairi ka Murgh is another seasonal speciality when raw mangoes are available. Lucknow cuisine is well known for the seasonal variation of its many dishes.

DAHI CHICKEN
(CHICKEN IN YOGHURT)

SERVES: 8   PREPARATION TIME: 1 HOUR

INGREDIENTS

Chicken	1 kg, cut into 12 pieces
Dahi (yoghurt)	1 kg
Onions	1 kg, grated
Adhrak (ginger)	2-inch piece, finely julienned
Maida (refined flour)	1 tbsp, for marination
Laung (cloves)	4 cloves
Kaali mirch (black peppercorns)	8 peppercorns
Sabut laal mirch (dried red chilli)	6, whole
Badi elaichi (black cardamom)	2 pods
Dalchini (cinnamon)	2 sticks, each broken into two
Kashmiri mirch (chilli)	2 tbsp (for the colour)
Ghee	4 tbsp
Salt	1 tsp or to taste

METHOD

Beat the yoghurt and mix it in with the chicken. Sprinkle the flour over this mixture. Mix well and let it marinate in the fridge for 6 hours.

Heat the ghee and sauté the grated onions and the ginger but do not allow them to brown. Then add all the whole masalas. Cook for 5 minutes.

Remove from the fire and add the Kashmiri chilli. The mixture should become pink in colour. Add the chicken mixture, then the salt and allow it to cook on a low flame, stirring continuously, until it comes to a boil. If this process is not followed the yoghurt will curdle.

Cook the chicken (with the mixture of onions) until it is tender and the yoghurt sticks to it. Serve hot with Methi ki Roti (see page 146 under Rotis).

MURGH-E-MUSALLAM
(MASALA CHICKEN)

SERVES: 8   PREPARATION TIME: 1 HOUR

INGREDIENTS

Whole chicken	1, approx. 800–900 gms, dressed
Dahi (yoghurt)	1 cup
Onions	250 gms, sliced
Badaam (almonds)	100 gms, blanched and coarsely slivered
Adhrak-lahsun (ginger-garlic) paste	2 tbsp
Khus-khus (poppy seeds) paste	3 tbsp
Kachha papita (raw papaya) paste	2 tbsp
Hari elaichi (green cardamom)	6–8 pods
Dalchini (cinnamon)	1-inch stick
Deghi mirch or Kashmiri mirch powder	2 tsp (for the colour)
Garam masala (ground spices) powder	2 tsp, heaped
Laal mirch (red chilli) powder	1 tsp
Dhania (coriander) powder	3 tsp
Haldi (turmeric) powder	1 tsp
Desiccated coconut	1 tbsp, heaped
Kewra (screw pine) water	3 drops
Kesar (saffron)	4–5 strands soaked in ½ tsp of warmed milk
Tejpatta (bay leaf)	2–3 leaves
Chandi ka varq (silver)	2–3 leaves
Slivered almonds	2 tbsp, for garnish
Refined oil	1 cup
Salt	1½ tsp or to taste

METHOD

Wash the chicken and pat dry the moisture with a paper towel. Thoroughly pierce the chicken with a fork. Generously rub the papaya paste and the ginger and garlic paste with salt. Let it marinate overnight.

Truss the chicken and tie the wings, neck and the legs together with twine.

In a large frying pan, heat ½ a cup of oil and fry the bay leaves, cardamoms and cinnamon until they start to sputter. Then on a high flame, fry the trussed chicken to a golden brown colour. Remove the chicken and put it aside to cool. In the same oil, lightly brown the onions and coarsely grind them to a paste.

In a bowl, mix all of the ingredients except the saffron and whip it into a thick batter-like consistency. Apply half of this paste to the chicken, filling the cavity as well as the undersides of the wings and the legs.

Take a heavy-bottomed pan and cook the remaining batter until it starts releasing an aroma. Add the saffron, mix well and pour this mixture over the trussed chicken. Serve hot, garnished with the silver leaves and the slivered almonds.

Note: The Murgh-e-Musallam can also be stuffed with 4 hard-boiled eggs that have been finely chopped and added to the mixture.

MURGH WAJID ALI
(SPICED CHICKEN BREASTS)

This dish is named after Nawab Wajid Ali Shah of Awadh.

SERVES: 12   PREPARATION TIME: 2 HOURS

INGREDIENTS FOR MARINATION AND FILLING

Chicken breasts	12 deboned, washed and flattened
Onions	1 cup, finely chopped
Adhrak (ginger)	2 tbsp, finely chopped
Hari mirch (green chilli)	5 pieces, slit, deseeded and finely chopped
Hara dhania (coriander)	12 leaves, finely chopped
Adhrak (ginger) paste	4 tsp
Lahsun (garlic) paste	4 tsp
Peeli mirch (yellow chilli) powder	½ tsp
Garam masala (ground spices)	½ tsp
Khoya	¾ cup
Lemon juice	2 tbsp
Salt	2 tbsp

METHOD

To marinate the flattened chicken breasts, rub them in a mixture of the ginger and garlic pastes mixed with the yellow chilli powder, garam masala and salt. Keep aside for 1 hour.

In a medium-sized bowl crumble the khoya, add all the chopped ingredients with 1 tablespoon of salt and the lemon juice and mix well. On a flat platter, divide the mixture into 12 equal portions.

To stuff each breast, place a portion of the mixture on it and roll it tightly with a twine. Grease a roasting tray and arrange the stuffed chicken breasts on it. In an oven preheated to 300°F/150°C, lightly roast the chicken breasts to a golden colour.

INGREDIENTS FOR THE GRAVY

Dahi (yoghurt)	1 cup
Onions	2 medium, finely chopped
Ginger paste	4 tsp
Garlic paste	4 tsp
Coconut	6 tsp, grated
Cashew nuts	½ cup, coarsely chopped
Almonds	24 almonds, blanched, peeled and halved
Garam masala (ground spices)	1 tsp
Desi ghee	½ cup
Salt	1 tsp
Kesar (saffron)	8 strands, soaked in 1 tbsp of warmed milk

METHOD

Heat the ghee in a pateela. Over a medium flame, sauté the onions in the ghee. Add the ginger and garlic pastes and sauté until their moisture reduces. Add the cashew nuts and the grated coconut, brown for 5 minutes. Lower the flame, add the yoghurt and simmer for 5 minutes. Then add the garam masala and salt, stirring continuously. Finally, add 4 strands of saffron and stir them in.

Into this gravy, carefully add the chicken breasts, one by one, and let them simmer until they are tender and coated evenly with the gravy. Serve the chicken breasts laid out in a flat dish in a single layer. Garnish with the blanched almonds and the remaining saffron poured over the chicken breasts.

MURGH ZAFFRANI
(SAFFRON CHICKEN)

SERVES: 8   PREPARATION TIME: 2 HOURS

INGREDIENTS

Chicken	900 gms–1 kg, skinned and cut into 12 pieces
Kesar (saffron) powder	1½ tsp
Onion	1 medium, thickly sliced
Adhrak (ginger)	3 pieces, coarsely chopped
Lahsun (garlic)	8 cloves
Dahi (yoghurt)	1 cup
Double cream	4 tbsp
Chironji (charoli)	¼ cup
Kaju (cashew nuts)	¼ cup
Hari elaichi (cardamom) powder	2 tsp
Kashmiri laal mirch (red chilli) powder	1½ tsp
Javitri (mace) powder	½ tsp
Kewra (screw pine) water	1 tbsp
Desi ghee	1½ cup
Sukhi laal mirch (dried red chilli)	4 medium-sized, fried
Salt	to taste
Charcoal	3–4 pieces, for the dum

METHOD

In a large platter, marinate the chicken with the yoghurt, double cream, chilli powder, mace and ½ a cup of ghee and mix it well. The chicken should be coated evenly with the marinade. Keep aside for an hour.

In a pan over medium flame, heat 1 cup of the ghee and fry the onions until they are well browned, ensuring that they do not burn. Transfer the onions onto a paper towel to drain any excess oil. Let them cool. Then grind the onions to make a paste.

In a large heavy-bottomed pot, add the onion paste, tightly cover the pot with a lid and set aside. Grind the garlic and ginger into a paste and add it to the pot with the onion paste.

In ⅓ cup of lukewarm water, make a paste of the cashew nuts and chironji and add to the mixture in the pot. Then add the chicken marinade to the pot along with the saffron, screw pine water and green cardamom and let it rest for 15 minutes. Cook this on a low flame with salt for another 15 minutes, stirring occasionally.

Then cover the pot with a heavy lid and seal the sides with kneaded dough. On the lid, place a metal bowl with 3 pieces of burning charcoal, making a dum and let it cook for 1 hour, or until the chicken becomes tender. Serve hot, garnished with whole red chillies.

DHANIA MURGH KA KORMA
(CHICKEN IN CORIANDER CURRY)

SERVES: 8   PREPARATION TIME: 30 MINUTES

INGREDIENTS

Chicken	1 chicken, cut into 12 pieces
Hara dhania (coriander) leaves	250 gms, finely chopped
Dahi (yoghurt)	1 kg, well-beaten
Onions	2 large, finely chopped
Lahsun (garlic)	1 tsp, ground
Saunf (fennel) powder	1 tbsp
Dalchini (cinnamon)	2 sticks
Hari elaichi (green cardamom)	4 pods
Laung (cloves)	6 cloves
Haldi (turmeric) powder	½ tsp
Sunflower oil	1 cup
Salt	1 tbsp or to taste

METHOD

Heat the oil in a frying pan, add the chicken pieces with the garlic paste and fry until the chicken turns a golden brown. Keep aside.

Sauté the onions until lightly browned. Lower the flame and add the beaten yoghurt, stirring continuously, until the oil rises to the surface. Add the turmeric, fennel powder, cinnamon, green cardamom, cloves and chopped coriander leaves and cook for 5–7 minutes.

To this mixture, add the fried chicken and salt and cook on a low flame until the chicken is tender and the gravy starts to reduce, thickens and coats the chicken. Serve hot.

KAIRI KA MURGH
(CHICKEN WITH RAW GREEN MANGOES)

SERVES: 12   PREPARATION TIME: 1 HOUR

INGREDIENTS

Chicken	1 cut into 12 pieces
Kaccha aam (raw green mangoes)	2 medium, cut lengthwise into 1½-inch pieces
Onions	3 medium, finely sliced
Adhrak (ginger) paste	½ tsp
Lahsun (garlic) paste	½ tsp
Laal mirch (red chilli) powder	¾ tsp
Hari mirch (green chilli)	2 pieces
Haldi (turmeric) powder	1 tsp
Oil	⅓ cup
Salt	1 tsp or to taste

METHOD

In a frying pan, heat 2 tablespoons of oil and fry the chicken pieces for about 5 minutes. Add the green chillies, ½ a teaspoon of turmeric and cook in ½ a cup of water until the chicken becomes tender. Keep aside.

Heat the remaining oil in another pan. Then, fry the onions until they turn a golden brown. Add the ginger and garlic pastes, ½ teaspoon of turmeric, the red chilli powder and salt. Fry for 2 minutes. Then add

3 tablespoons of water, cover and cook on a low flame for a couple of minutes to blend in the spices.

Add the chicken and the raw mango slices. Cook on a low flame for about 5–10 minutes. This dish is semi-dry. Serve hot.

CHICKEN ROAST IN YOGHURT

SERVES: 4   PREPARATION TIME: 30 MINUTES

INGREDIENTS

Chicken	1 kg, broiler
Dahi (yoghurt)	½ cup
Onions	4–5 small, finely chopped
Adhrak-lahsun (ginger-garlic) paste	1 tsp
Mushroom	100 gms, halved
Shimla mirch (capsicum)	1 large, sliced
Vinegar	1 tbsp
Sunflower oil	2 tbsp
Salt	1 tsp or to taste

METHOD

Marinate the chicken in the ginger and garlic paste, yoghurt and salt overnight in a refrigerator.

Cook the chicken in a pan with the marinade. Add the vinegar and brown slowly on a low flame, until the chicken is tender.

Heat the oil in another pan and lightly brown the onions. Add the chicken, sprinkle some water over it and keep stirring, so that it gets evenly browned. Then fry on a high flame until the water gets absorbed.

In a small frying pan, heat 1 tablespoon of oil and sauté the sliced capsicum and halved mushrooms until they become tender. Add this to the chicken mixture and let it blend in for 3 minutes. Serve hot.

CHICKEN À LA SCALA

SERVES: 8   PREPARATION TIME: 1 HOUR

INGREDIENTS

Chicken	1 kg, quartered
Long spaghetti	250 gms
Onion	1 large
Carrot	1 large, sliced
Egg	1 yolk
Mushrooms	250 gms, thinly sliced
Refined flour	¼ cup
Cream	3 tsp
Tabasco (optional)	few drops
Tejpatta (bay leaf)	2 leaves
Kaali mirch (Black peppercorns)	6 peppercorns
Cloves	4 cloves
Cheese	3 tbsp, strong, grated hard cheese
Butter	6 tbsp, melted
Salt	1 tsp

METHOD

Cook the chicken in a pressure cooker with the onion, bay leaves, carrot, peppercorns, cloves and salt for one whistle. Once cooled remove the chicken, debone it and dice it into squares.

In a frying pan, melt 4 tablespoons of butter, add the flour and cook for a minute. Then add the stock in which the chicken had been cooked in the pressure cooker.

In a separate pan, heat 2 tablespoons of butter and sauté the mushrooms. Beat the egg yolk lightly with a few drops of tabasco and add this to the white butter sauce. Stir in the mushrooms, cream and the diced chicken. Reheat without bringing it to a boil.

Cook the spaghetti in plenty of salted boiling water. Put in a colander and let all the excess water drain out. Then place alternate layers of the spaghetti and the chicken in a well-buttered glass casserole. Sprinkle it with grated cheese and butter. Bake in a hot oven at 350°F/180°C for 10 minutes. Serve hot with steamed rice.

Note: It is not necessary to bake this dish. Alternatively, cheese may be added to the hot mixture so that it melts.

CHICKEN CHASSEUR

SERVES: 4   PREPARATION TIME: 30 MINUTES

INGREDIENTS

Chicken	1 kg broiler, cut into 4 pieces, deboned
Maida (refined flour)	6 tbsp
Onions	2 medium, thinly sliced
Mushrooms	100 gms, sliced
Tomatoes	250 gms, skinned and chopped
Chicken sausages	4 sausages (optional)
Salt	to taste

For the Sauce

Chicken stock	2 cups
Rosemary	1 tsp, dried and ground
Parsley	2 sprigs
Kaali mirch (black peppercorns)	½ tsp, freshly ground
Tejpatta (bay leaf)	2 leaves
Butter	1½ cups
Salt	to taste

METHOD

Coat the chicken well with 5 tablespoons of flour mixed with salt. Heat 2½ tablespoons of butter in a saucepan. Fry the chicken until golden brown. Remove and put into a casserole.

Heat the remaining butter in a pan, add the onions and sauté until soft. Add the mushrooms and tomatoes. Sauté for a few minutes. Put these in the casserole. (You may also add sausages.)

For the sauce, make a paste of the remaining flour with the butter and a little water and add to the chicken stock along with the rosemary, parsley, bay leaves, black pepper and salt. Cook until the sauce thickens slightly and then pour over the chicken and the vegetable mixture.

Cover the casserole and cook in a moderately hot oven (350°F/180°C) for 1½ hours. Serve hot.

Fish

When my mother arrived in Lucknow, she was delighted to discover that a dish named Balochi Machhli was made by the main cook of Government House. Being from Quetta, she soon popularized this fish recipe among her friends.

Lahori Machhli came down from Lahore, where their bawarchees (cooks) marinated rahu, a sweet river fish which was found in abundance in the Darya-e-Ravi from autumn to spring. Lahori Machhli is cooked to perfection in aromatic spices. Ironically, fish was considered a poor man's food. Today, the wealthy enjoy it more.

A healthy variation for weight-watchers is Dum ki Machhli (steamed fish fillets). These are lightly fried in yoghurt and then dum cooked to infuse all the flavours.

India has innumerable recipes of fish curries, with many regional varieties. Machhli ka Saalan or the fish curry that is made in Lucknow is the regional speciality.

Our house specialities are Masala Fish and Soya Fish. The former is a shallow-fried fish, seasoned with spices and chillies. The latter dish consists of fish that is cooked in mustard and fresh soya leaves that give it a very palatable zest. For years, my mother has been preparing the most delicious fish that is cooked only in tomatoes and garlic. Fried sole fillets are another simple way of cooking sole, which is a delectable river fish found in the Gomti River.

BALOCHI MACHHLI

INGREDIENTS

Fish (singhada)	1 kg
Pudina (mint) leaves	½ bunch
Dhania (coriander)	1 bunch, fresh
Hari mirch (green chilli)	4–6 pieces
Lahsun (garlic) paste	2 tbsp
Atta (wheat flour)	2 tbsp
Vinegar	4 tbsp
Sabut laal mirch (whole dried red chilli)	2 tbsp, crushed
Haldi (turmeric) powder	1 tsp
Sukhi adhrak (dry ginger) powder	1 tsp
Jeera (cumin) seeds	2 tbsp
Saunf (fennel) seeds	1 tbsp
Ajwain (caraway) seeds	1 tsp
Sunflower oil	2 cups, for frying
Lime Juice	4 tbsp
Salt	1 tsp or to taste

METHOD

Soak the fish in lime juice and salt for 10 minutes. Then wash the fish thoroughly under running water and keep it in the freezer for 10 minutes (this helps to slice the fish thinly). Remove and cut into thin slices.

Lightly roast the cumin seeds, fennel seeds, caraway seeds and dry ginger powder on a griddle. Remove from the flame and grind finely. Make a paste of green chillies, coriander and mint with vinegar. Mix both these mixtures together and add the dried red chilli, salt, turmeric, garlic paste and wheat flour with 2 tablespoons of oil. Add a little water to make a paste. Marinate the fish slices in this paste and refrigerate for one hour.

Heat the oil in a kadhai on a medium flame for 5 minutes. Then deep-fry the fish until it is crisp. Serve hot.

LAHORI MACHHLI

SERVES: 8   PREPARATION TIME: 40 MINUTES

INGREDIENTS

Fish (surmai or rohu)	1 kg, cut into boneless fillets
Rice water	4 cups
Rice flour	2 tbsp
Besan (gram flour)	1 cup, sifted
Limes	4–6 juiced
Garam masala (ground spices)	1 tbsp
Laal mirch (whole red chillies)	1 tbsp, crushed
Jeera (cumin) seeds	1 tsp, roasted and powdered
Ajwain (caraway) seeds	½ tsp
Haldi (turmeric) powder	1 tsp
Oil	3 cups, for deep-frying
Salt	1 tbsp or to taste

Note: Make the rice water by boiling 1 tablespoon of rice in 4 cups of water. Strain and save the water.

METHOD

Soak the fish fillets in lime juice or vinegar and salt for 10 minutes. Then thoroughly wash under running water.

Mix the turmeric and the juice of 3 limes with the rice water. Mix the gram flour and rice flour with all the spices and the salt.

Dip each piece of fish in the rice water. Then apply the gram flour mixture to it with a halved lime. Coat all the fish pieces with the gram flour mixture. Leave for half an hour.

Heat the oil in a kadhai (Indian wok) then deep-fry the fish on a high flame until it turns golden brown. Remove the fish from the kadhai with a strainer and immediately sprinkle a pinch of gram flour on it. Serve hot.

DUM KI MACHHLI
(TRADITIONAL STEAMED FISH)

SERVES: 8   PREPARATION TIME: 25 MINUTES

INGREDIENTS

Fish (singhada)	1 kg, cut into fillets of 3-inch size
Onions	4 medium, ground
Haldi (turmeric) powder	½ tsp
Adhrak (ginger) paste	1 tsp
Lahsun (garlic) paste	1 tsp
Hari mirch (green chillies)	10 pieces, deseeded and ground
Magaz (watermelon and musk melon)	1 tbsp, ground
Tarbuz (watermelon) seeds	1 tbsp, ground
Shahi jeera (black cumin) seeds	1 tsp
Dalchini (cinnamon) stick	1 inch long
Laung (cloves)	8 cloves
Dahi (yoghurt)	2-2½ cups, beaten
Oil	1¼ cups
Salt	1 tsp or to taste

METHOD

Heat the oil. Sauté the whole spices for a couple of minutes, then add the ground onions and fry the paste until it turns golden brown. Add the ginger and garlic paste, green chillies, turmeric and salt. Fry for a minute and then add the yoghurt. Stir continuously and cook on a medium flame until it comes to a boil. Add the ground musk melon and watermelon seeds and slide the mixture into the fish fillets.

Cover and simmer the fish for about 10 minutes, gently stirring a few times, ensuring that the fillets do not break. Cook until the fish becomes tender. A little water can be added while the fish is being cooked to get the required consistency of the gravy. The dish has a medium to thick gravy. Serve hot.

MACHHLI MUSSALAM
(WHOLE FISH WITH SPICES)

SERVES: 8   PREPARATION TIME: 1½ HOURS

INGREDIENTS

Fish river sole	1 kg, cleaned and deboned
Dahi (yoghurt)	1 cup, to cover the fish
Onion	½ cup, paste
Onion	2, 1 sliced and 1 deep-fried
Adhrak (ginger) paste	2 tbsp
Lahsun (garlic) paste	2 tbsp
Hari mirch (green chilli)	6 sliced and deseeded
Laal mirch (red chilli) powder	1 tsp
Haldi (turmeric) powder	1 tsp
Methi (fenugreek) seeds	1 tsp
Garam masala (ground spices)	1 tsp
Lime juice	1 tbsp
Kewra (screw pine) water	3 drops
Sunflower oil	1 cup
Water	1 cup
Salt	1 tsp
Til (sesame) oil	2 tbsp

METHOD

Rub the fish with lime salt juice or vinegar. Keep aside for 10 minutes. Then wash it thoroughly under running water.

Prepare a marinade with 1 tablespoon each of the ginger and garlic pastes, 1 tablespoon of lemon juice, the red chilli powder, turmeric and salt with the yoghurt and the sesame oil. Prick the fish with a sharp fork, rub the marinade over it and let it marinate for 1 hour.

Separately, grind one of the sliced onions to a fine paste, along with the fried onion, the green chillies and the remaining ginger and garlic pastes.

Heat the oil in a large flat pan, fry the fenugreek seeds. Add the onion paste and the prepared masala paste and let it brown. Then add the fish along with the marinade. Add a cup of water with the garam masala, cover and let it cook until all the water is almost absorbed. Then add the kewra water and cook until the fish is tender. Serve hot.

MACHHLI KA SAALAN
(FISH CURRY)

SERVES: 4   PREPARATION TIME: 30 MINUTES

INGREDIENTS

Fish river sole or rahu	1 kg, cut into 3-inch fillets
Onions	2 medium, finely sliced
Tomatoes	2 medium, grated, with the skin removed
Imli (tamarind)	1 tbsp, washed and deseeded
Adhrak (ginger)	1 tsp, grated
Lahsun (garlic)	1 tsp, crushed
Sukhi laal mirch (dried red chillies)	4 whole
Laal mirch (red chilli) powder	1 tsp
Haldi (turmeric) powder	½ tsp
Dhania (coriander) seeds	4 tsp
Jeera (cumin) seeds	2 tsp
Oil	1 cup
Salt	2 tsp or to taste

METHOD

Heat the oil and fry the onions until they turn golden brown. Add the ginger and garlic, all the spices and salt and fry for 5–7 minutes. Then sprinkle 2 tablespoons of water, cover and let it simmer for 5 minutes so that the spices blend together. Add the grated tomatoes and sauté them until the liquid is absorbed.

Then add ½ a cup of water into this mixture. When the water starts to boil, slide in the fish fillets. Cover and let them simmer, stirring occasionally and gently until the fish is cooked with its thick gravy. Serve hot with Zaffrani Pulao (see page 137 under Biryanis).

Kakori Kebab, Fish Kebab and Shami Kebab

Til ke Aloo, Bharwaan Shimla Mirch and
Bharwaan Karela with Aloo

Lachha Parantha and Palak Gosht

Irish Stew

Kairi Keema and Nargisi Kofta

Sheermal, Baqarkhani, Ultey Tawe ka Parantha and
Murgh Mussalam

Fish in Tomato and Garlic Sauce

Karele ki Sabzi, Khatti Arhar ki Dal and Kala Chana with Kadhai Paneer

Anaar ka Raita and Subzion ki Tehri

Burhani Raita, Kachoombar Salad, Pudina Chutney and Gosht Biryani

Phirni, Rabarhi and Aam Malai

Stewed Guava with Cream and Jalebi Pudding

Chocolate Mayonnaise Cake with Fudge Frosting, Basic Sponge Cake,
Aloo ki Tikki and Korma Sandwiches

Keema, Matar and Aloo Samosas

SOYA FISH

SERVES: 8   PREPARATION TIME: 1 HOUR

INGREDIENTS

Fish pomfret (cheetal)/catfish (singhada)	1 kg
Fresh soya	2 kg, bunch
Tomatoes	2 medium, grated
Onions	2 medium, finely chopped
Lime juice/Vinegar	1 tbsp
Lahsun (garlic) paste	1 tbsp
Adhrak (ginger) paste	1 tbsp
Kaali sarson (black mustard) paste	1 tbsp, freshly ground
Garam masala (ground spices)	1 tbsp
Haldi (turmeric) powder	1 tsp
Laal mirch (chilli) powder	1 tsp
Dhania (coriander) powder	1 tsp
Sabut laal mirch (dried red chilli)	5 whole
Egg	1 beaten
Maida (wheat flour)	2 tbsp
Soya sauce	2 tsp
Sunflower oil	4 tbsp
Salt	1 tbsp or to taste

METHOD

Cut the fish into 2-inch pieces and soak in lime juice or vinegar for 5 minutes. Then wash under running water.

In a large bowl, beat the flour, egg, turmeric powder and salt. Add the fish pieces to this mixture and set aside for 15 minutes for it to marinate. In a heated frying pan, deep-fry the fish to form a fritter-like texture. Take the pieces out and let them cool and soak the excess oil on a kitchen paper towel.

Pick the soya leaves off the stems and chop them coarsely. Wash them under running water.

Finely chop the onions and fry them in a pan until they are well browned. Add the ginger and garlic pastes, the black mustard paste and the grated tomatoes to this mixture. Mix all the masalas together in a bowl with ½ a cup of water and add these masalas to the onion-tomato mixture and cook until the oil rises to the surface.

Add the coarsely chopped soya leaves and cook for 10 minutes. The liquid will reduce to a quarter of its original quantity. Then add the soya sauce and 1 cup of water until it is a reduced curry which can coat the fish evenly. Add the whole red chillies and the fried fillets to this curry and keep it aside for 10–15 minutes so that the fried fish soaks in the soya curry. The soya fish is ready to be served hot.

MACHHLI MASALA
(MASALA FISH)

SERVES: 8   PREPARATION TIME: 1 HOUR

INGREDIENTS

Sole fish	1 kg, cut into 3-inch pieces
Onions	2 medium, fried and ground to a paste
Lahsun (garlic) paste	1 tbsp
Adhrak (ginger) paste	1 tbsp
Hari mirch (green chilli)	4 deseeded and finely chopped
Laal mirch (red chilli) powder	1 tsp
Haldi (turmeric) powder	1 tsp
Methi (fenugreek) seeds	1 tsp
Jeera (cumin) powder	1 tsp
Dhania (coriander) powder	1 tsp
Lime juice/Vinegar	2 tbsp
Desi ghee	1 cup
Salt	2 tsp or to taste

METHOD

Cut the fish into 3-inch pieces and soak them in lime juice or vinegar for 5 minutes. Then wash under running water.

Marinate the fish in the ginger and garlic pastes, with the green chillies, fenugreek seeds, all the powdered spices and salt for 2 hours.

In a large flat pan, heat the desi ghee on a medium flame and fry the onion paste until it turns golden brown. In this ghee, shallow-fry the marinated fish. Serve hot with onion rings.

FISH IN TOMATO AND GARLIC SAUCE

SERVES: 8   PREPARATION TIME: 30 MINUTES

INGREDIENTS

Fish	8 medium-sized fillets of sole or any good white river fish
Onion	½ kg, finely chopped
Tomatoes	½ kg, finely chopped
Snow mountain garlic/ Ek pothi lahsun (garlic)	1 whole bulb, cloves separated and fried whole for garnishing
Garlic	1 whole bulb, separated, peeled and chopped
Lahsun (garlic) paste	1 tbsp
Onion paste	1 tbsp
Kaali mirch (Black peppercorns)	12 whole
Black pepper powder	1 tsp
Tejpatta (Bay leaf)	3 leaves
Hari mirch (Green chilli)	4 pieces
Badaam (Almonds)	10 blanched, peeled and separated into halves
Sunflower oil	½ cup
Salt	1 tsp or to taste

METHOD

Cut the fish into 3-inch fillets and soak them in lime juice or vinegar for 10 minutes. Then wash under clean running water.

Heat the oil in a pan, add the onion and garlic pastes with black peppercorns and bay leaves and sauté for 3 minutes. Add and sauté the chopped cloves of garlic with the chopped onions, without allowing them to brown. Then add the chopped tomatoes with the black pepper powder and salt. Allow the mixture to simmer to reduce the water content from the tomatoes. Slide the fish fillets into the gravy. Cook for 10–15 minutes, until the fish is tender.

Serve hot. Before serving, gently mix in the fried snow mountain garlic cloves, green chillies and garnish with the blanched and halved almonds.

FRIED SOLE FILLETS

SERVES: 8   PREPARATION TIME: 1 HOUR

INGREDIENTS

Sole/pomfret fillets	8 fillets
Adhrak-lahsun (ginger-garlic) paste	1 tbsp
Maida (refined flour)	1 tbsp
Eggs	2 egg whites, whisked
Bread	½ cup, fresh bread without the sides
Kaali mirch (black pepper) powder	1 tsp
Refined oil	3 cups, for deep-frying
Lime juice	1 tbsp
Salt	1 tsp

METHOD

Soak the fish fillets in lime juice or vinegar for 5 minutes. Then wash under running water.

Marinate the fish in ginger and garlic paste, salt and black pepper for an hour. Roll the fillets in the whisked egg whites and maida mixture and finally coat them with bread. Keep aside for 10 minutes for the bread to stick to the fillets.

Heat the oil in a wok (kadhai) and deep-fry the fillets until golden brown. Remove with a perforated spoon and drain the excess oil on paper towels. Serve immediately with French fries and mixed salad leaves with dressing.

Dals and Lentils

Lucknow's favourite lentils are Arhar ki Dal and Chane ki Dal. These are the most common among all available lentils. Every house has its own particular way of cooking them. The recipes in this cookbook are the way we cook them in our kitchens.

Kaala Chana with Kadhai Paneer is a house speciality, where boiled black chickpeas are cooked with milk that is freshly curdled on the pan itself. This dish is quick and unusual.

Lucknow ki Karhi is distinctly different to the karhis that are cooked in neighbouring states. It is a speciality of Lucknow, particularly in vegetarian homes.

Lucknow also specializes in using Chane ki Dal with eggs and with mutton. A vegetarian version is cooked with lauki (bottle gourd). All these appetizing dishes are simple and nutritious.

KHATTI ARHAR KI DAL

SERVES: 8   PREPARATION TIME: 30 MINUTES

INGREDIENTS

Arhar dal (Toor dal)	1 cup
Onions	1 medium, finely chopped
Adhrak-lahsun (ginger-garlic) paste	1 tbsp
Imli (tamarind) paste	⅓ cup
Sabut laal mirch (red chilli)	7 whole
Haldi powder (turmeric)	1 tsp
Garam masala (ground spices)	1 tsp
Karhi patta (curry leaves)	20 small leaves
Kachhi moongfali (raw peanuts)	2/3 cup
Oil	3 tbsp
Salt	1 tbsp or to taste

METHOD

Wash the dal properly, transfer to a cooker, cover and cook. After half a whistle, take it off the flame.

Soak the peanuts in water for one hour.

Heat the oil in a kadhai. Put in the curry leaves and then fry the finely chopped onions until light brown, add red chilli, ginger and garlic paste, turmeric powder, garam masala powder, tamarind paste and mix the dal with the masala mixture.

Then add salt as per taste, cook for a minute and add the raw peanuts. Khatti Arhar ki Dal is ready to be served.

CHANE KI DAL WITH LAUKI
(BENGAL GRAM WITH SQUASH)

SERVES: 8   PREPARATION TIME: 1½ HOURS

INGREDIENTS

Chana dal (Bengal gram)	1 cup, well washed
Lauki (squash)	250 gms, peeled and chopped into

	1-inch squares
Tomatoes	2 medium, chopped
Onion	1 medium, sliced
Jeera (cumin) seeds	½ tsp
Adhrak (fresh ginger)	1-inch piece, grated
Laal mirch (red chilli) powder	¼ tsp
Haldi (turmeric) powder	¼ tsp
Dhania (coriander) leaves	8 fresh leaves, for garnishing
Oil/Desi ghee	1 tbsp/2 tbsp
Salt	1–2 tsp or to taste

METHOD

Heat the oil in a saucepan and sauté the onions. Add the cumin seeds and cook for a couple of minutes, until the seeds start to sputter. Add the tomatoes, ginger, red chilli, turmeric and salt and cook over a low flame for about 5 minutes.

Add the lauki to the mixture and cook for 10 to 15 minutes. Then add the chana dal with 1 cup of water. Cover the saucepan and let it simmer for approximately 45 minutes or until the dal is well blended and thoroughly cooked. Before serving, garnish with freshly chopped coriander leaves.

KAALA CHANA WITH KADHAI PANEER
(BLACK CHICKPEAS WITH FRESH COTTAGE CHEESE)

SERVES: 8

PREPARATION TIME: 2 HOURS

COOKING TIME: 15 MINUTES

INGREDIENTS

Kaala chana (black chickpeas)	500 gms, soaked for 2 hrs and boiled
Paneer	250 gms, freshly made in a kadhai (wok)
Lime	2, juiced
Red chilli flakes	pinch
Sabut laal mirch (dried red chillies)	3 whole
Onions	3 medium, finely chopped
Haldi (turmeric) powder	1 tsp

Laal mirch (red chilli) powder	1 tsp
Dhania (coriander) powder	1½ tsp
Sabzi masala	2 tsp
Hari mirch (green chilli)	3 whole, slit on one side and deseeded
Hara dhania (coriander)	2 sprigs, finely chopped
Vegetable oil	3 tbsp, for frying
Salt	1 tsp

METHOD

For fresh cottage cheese:

1 litre of milk makes 250 grams of paneer.

In a kadhai, boil the milk, then take it off the fire and add the juice of 2 limes for the milk to separate. Put it back on the fire and let it cook until the milk starts to form lumps of fresh cheese. To this add salt to taste and a pinch of red chilli flakes. Finally, add 3 whole dried red chillies.

For the Kaala Chana:

Heat the oil and brown the onions. Then add the other masalas with the salt. Add the boiled black chickpeas and paneer and cook for 10 minutes. A minute before turning off the heat, add the whole green chillies with the freshly chopped coriander leaves. The dish is ready to be served.

LUCKNOW KI KARHI

SERVES: 8   PREPARATION TIME: 20 MINUTES

INGREDIENTS

Dahi (yoghurt)	1 kg
Besan (gram flour)	2 tbsp
Lahsun (garlic) paste	1 tsp
Hari mirch (green chillies)	6 small
Sabut laal mirch (dried red chilli)	4 whole
Haldi (turmeric) powder	½ tsp
Dhania (coriander) powder	½ tsp

Jeera (cumin) powder	½ tsp
Methi (fenugreek) seeds	¼ tsp
Kaali sarson (black mustard) seeds	1 tsp
Karhi patta (curry leaves)	20 small leaves
Onions	3 medium, finely chopped
Oil	3 tbsp
Salt	1 tbsp or to taste

METHOD

In a large heavy-bottomed pan, beat 1 kilogram of yoghurt with 500 millilitres of water. Slowly add the gram flour and blend together ensuring that it is lump-free.

Heat the oil in a heavy-bottomed pan and add one finely chopped onion, garlic paste, mustard seeds, cumin powder, fenugreek seeds, whole red chillies, curry leaves, green chillies and salt. Sauté this mixture until it turns golden. On a slow flame add the mixed yoghurt, gradually stirring until the karhi comes to a boil. After one boil, let it simmer for an hour on a low flame.

FOR PAKORIS:

Besan (gram flour)	100 gms
Oil	200 ml
Hara dhania (coriander) leaves	2 tsp, freshly chopped
Onions	1 finely chopped
Hari mirch (green chillies)	2 finely chopped
Baking powder	¼ tsp
Salt	1 tsp

METHOD

Make a mixture of these ingredients and let it rest for 10 minutes. The consistency of the mixture should be thick enough to coat the onions and to form small pakodis (round balls).

For deep-frying, heat the oil on a high flame in a heavy-bottomed pan. Then collect the mixture together with your fingers and drop it into the pan, one by one. They should form small pakodis. As they turn golden and start rising upwards, take them out with a perforated frying spoon and keep aside.

Add these pakodis to the prepared karhi and let them cook together for 10 more minutes. The karhi is ready to be tempered with the remaining 2 medium-sized onions finely chopped and well browned in oil or desi ghee and then poured on top of the karhi. Serve hot with steamed rice.

CHANE KI DAL WITH ANDA
(SPLIT BENGAL GRAM WITH EGGS)

SERVES: 8

PREPARATION TIME: 3 HOURS

COOKING TIME: 30 MINUTES

INGREDIENTS

Eggs	8 hard-boiled and halved
Chana dal (split Bengal gram)	2½ cups
Onions	6 medium, 2 chopped, 4 ground to a paste
Lahsun (garlic)	1 tsp, ground to a paste
Adhrak (ginger)	2 tsp, ground to a paste
Hari mirch (green chilli)	2–3 pieces
Haldi (turmeric) powder	1 tsp
Dhania (coriander) powder	1 tsp
Jeera (cumin) powder	1 tsp
Laal mirch (red chilli) powder	1 tbsp
Garam masala (ground spices) powder	½ tsp
Tejpatta (bay leaf)	1 leaf
Sugar	1 tsp
Oil	⅓ cup
Desi ghee	2 tbsp
Fresh coriander leaves	12 leaves, finely chopped
Salt	2 tsp

Optional: Before adding the egg halves, coat them lightly with whipped gram flour and a pinch of red chilli powder. Lightly fry in very hot oil.

METHOD

Soak the dal for 3 hours and drain.

Fry 2 chopped onions in oil until they turn light brown. Add the ground onion and the ginger and garlic pastes and fry for a few minutes. Add the bay leaf and fry well with all the powdered spices, except the garam masala.

In a pan, add the dal, salt and sugar and cook for 15 minutes until the dal is tender. Add the green chillies and then cover the pan and cook for 5 more minutes. If the gravy is too thick add water accordingly and let it boil. Then add the ghee and garam masala along with the eggs and cook for 1 minute. Garnish with fresh coriander leaves. Serve with steamed basmati rice.

DAL GOSHT
(MUTTON COOKED WITH LENTILS)

SERVES: 6–8

PREPARATION TIME: 2 HOURS

COOKING TIME: 40 MINUTES

INGREDIENTS

Mutton	1 kg, 1 leg of raan cut into gol boti pieces
Chana dal (split Bengal gram)	1½ cups, soaked for 2 hours
Onions	3 medium, chopped and ground to a paste
Tomatoes	4 medium, chopped and ground to a paste
Dahi (yoghurt)	1 cup
Adhrak-lahsun (ginger-garlic) paste	4 tsp
Haldi (turmeric) powder	1 tsp
Laal mirch (red chilli) powder	2 tsp
Garam masala (ground spices) powder	2 tsp
Sugar	1 tsp
Fresh coriander leaves	12 leaves, finely chopped
Vegetable oil	6 tbsp
Salt	1 tbsp or to taste

METHOD

Drain and cook the chana dal in 1 cup of water until it is tender. Do not overcook. Drain and keep aside.

Heat the oil in a wok (kadhai). Add the mutton and fry until it is well browned. Add the ginger and garlic paste, turmeric powder, red chilli powder, garam masala and the onion and tomato pastes. Lower the flame and cook until the oil separates from the mixture.

In a separate pan, mix 2½ cups of water in the yoghurt. Add salt and sugar and then cook on low heat until the mutton is tender. Add the chana dal and bring it all to a boil. Lower the flame and let the dal simmer until it is well blended. Serve hot, garnished with freshly chopped coriander leaves.

Raitas

Yoghurt is popular throughout India and everybody makes their dahi (yoghurt) at home. Raita is a term used when yoghurt has different spices, vegetables and sometimes even fruit added to it that give it a flavour that could range from sweet to spicy. India abounds in regional specialities of raita. Burhani Raita, which traditionally accompanies a Gosht ki Biryani, is essentially Lucknowi. This garlic raita enhances and 'tames' the spiciness of this biryani. For decades, our Sunday lunch has been biryani with Burhani Raita and Kachoomber (cucumber) Salad with Pudina (mint) Chutney.

In our home, Anaar ka Raita is a speciality. This is made with red pomegranate arils that have been delicately spiced.

Lucknow's seasonal specialities among raitas is Kachnar ki Kali ka Raita. These Bauhinia buds, when in season, make the most delicate and healthy of raitas.

The Pahari/Desi Kheerey (cucumber) ka Raita and the Galgal aur Mooli (Kumaon lemon and radish) ka Raita recipes were given to me by my friend Ira Pande. Ira is a writer and an editor who is from Kumaon. Her mother, Shivani, was a famous Hindi writer. Ira wrote the most wonderful memoir of her mother and her writings titled *Diddi—My Mother's Voice*. Shivani had adopted Lucknow as her city. She lived there for thirty years and introduced and popularized many Kumaoni dishes in Lucknow. She was a superb cook and was known for the table she kept.

BURHANI RAITA
(SPICED YOGHURT)

SERVES: 8   PREPARATION TIME: 10 MINUTES

INGREDIENTS

Dahi (yoghurt)	2½ cups
Lahsun (garlic)	1 tbsp, crushed and juiced
Jeera (cumin) powder	½ tsp
Laal mirch (red chilli) powder	½ tsp
Salt	to taste

METHOD

Add salt to the crushed garlic. Add to the yoghurt and gently whip. Add the red chilli and cumin powders and mix them into the yoghurt.

Pour into a serving bowl. Before serving the raita, decorate it with a quarter teaspoon each of the red chilli powder and the cumin powder. The Burhani Raita is ready to be served.

Note: This raita is traditionally served with Mutton Biryani.

KACHNAR KI KALI KA RAITA
(RAITA WITH BAUHINIA FLOWER BUDS)

SERVES: 8   PREPARATION TIME: 15 MINUTES

INGREDIENTS

Dahi (yoghurt)	2½ cups, beaten
Kachnar ki kali (Bauhinia flower buds, when in season)	1½ cups
Onions	3 medium, finely sliced
Lahsun (garlic) paste	1 tsp
Haldi (turmeric) powder	¼ tsp
Laal mirch (red chilli) powder	1 tsp
Oil	⅔ cup
Salt	1 tsp or to taste

METHOD

Wash and soak the Bauhinia flower buds for 10 minutes. Keep aside.

Heat the oil in a medium-sized pan. Then add the sliced onions and fry them until they turn golden brown. Add the garlic, turmeric, red chilli powder and salt. Fry for 2 minutes. Sprinkle a little water, cover and simmer for 2 minutes for the spices to blend. Add the flower buds and sauté for a few minutes.

Then add the yoghurt and continue cooking for another 5 minutes, stirring continuously. Add 2 tablespoons of water, cover the pan and cook on a low flame, until the flower buds are tender and all the water is absorbed. The oil should rise to the surface. Serve hot.

PAHARI/DESI KHEEREY KA RAITA
(YOGHURT RAITA WITH CUCUMBER)

SERVES: 8   PREPARATION TIME: 15 MINUTES

INGREDIENTS

Pahari kheera (cucumber)/	1 medium/
Desi cucumber	4 large, peeled and grated
Dahi (yoghurt)	2 cups
Kaali sarson (black mustard) seeds	2 tsp, small seeds ground to a paste
Jeera (cumin) powder	2 tsp, freshly roasted
Salt	to taste

For Garnishing:

Hari mirch (green chilli)	4 pieces, deseeded and chopped
Fresh coriander leaves	12 leaves, freshly chopped
Laal mirch (red chilli) powder	½ tsp

METHOD

Grate the cucumbers and squeeze out the excess juice. Add the black mustard paste and let it release its pungent tang into the cucumbers for about 2–3 hours. Keep aside.

Grind the coriander leaves, green chillies and the red chilli powder into a paste. Just before serving, gently whip the yoghurt and add it to the coriander and chilli paste with the roasted cumin powder and salt. Keep aside some of the cumin powder for the garnish.

Before serving, garnish with the remaining cumin powder and some of the chopped fresh coriander leaves. Serve chilled.

GALGAL AUR MOOLI KA RAITA
(YOGHURT RAITA WITH KUMAON LEMON AND RADISH)

SERVES: 8   PREPARATION TIME: 15 MINUTES

INGREDIENTS

Dahi (yoghurt)	4 cups
Galgal (Kumaon lemons)/Kaffir limes/ Kinnows	2 with the sweet pith 8 peeled, pitted and seented
Mooli (radishes)	2 large, sweet and white, peeled and cut into short sticks
Bhang (cannabis) seeds*	½ cup
Dhania (coriander leaves)	20 leaves
Hari mirch (green chilli)	6 pieces
Salt and sugar	as per taste to balance the sweet-sour flavour of the raita

METHOD

In a large glass bowl, mix the radish sticks and Kumaon lime pith or substitute with kinnows. Grind the green coriander and green chillies together and mix in well with the radish and citrus fruit.

Roast the bhang seeds on a low flame in a non-stick pan (be careful as they tend to sputter). Let them cool, then grind and add to the spiced radish and fruit mixture.

Separately whisk the yoghurt, add the salt and sugar according to taste to balance the piquant sweet-and-sour flavour. Serve chilled, garnished with the freshly chopped coriander leaves.

---

*The non-intoxicant part of the cannabis plant, available only in Kumaon.

ANAAR KA RAITA
(POMEGRANATE YOGHURT)

SERVES: 8   PREPARATION TIME: 10 MINUTES

INGREDIENTS

Dahi (yoghurt)	2½ cups
Anaar (pomegranate)	1 whole fruit, arils deseeded
Jeera (cumin) powder	½ tsp
Laal mirch (red chilli) powder	½ tsp
Anaardana (pomegranate) seeds	1 tsp, finely crushed to a powder
Salt	to taste

METHOD

Gently whip the yoghurt. Mix the red chilli powder, cumin powder, salt and anaardana into the yoghurt. Pour into a serving bowl.

Before serving the raita, add the arils (fresh pomegranate seeds) and mix. Decorate the raita with a quarter teaspoon each of the red chilli and cumin powders. The Anaar ka Raita is ready. Serve chilled with biryanis and pulaos.

Biryanis and Pulaos

The difference between biryanis and pulaos has always been a controversial issue in Indian gastronomy. Both the dishes consist of long-grained rice cooked with vegetables, meat, poultry, seafood or fish.

However, there are a few general differences between these two types of rice preparations. Firstly, pulaos usually accompany a meal, whereas biryanis are the centrepiece of a meal, accompanied by various kinds of side dishes, mainly kebabs.

Secondly, pulaos are a single pot dish consisting of seven components—onions, meat, carrots, rice, salt, oil and water. This dish is prepared by sautéing the spices, then the meat, followed by rice in oil or desi ghee. Finally, the water is added and the mixture is simmered until all the water has been absorbed. Pulaos were favoured by aristocrats. Wealthy epicures fed musk and saffron pills to their chickens to scent their meat for the broth in which they prepared and simmered the rice.

Pulaos were given poetic names such as Noor (light), Moti (pearl) and Chameli (jasmine). Famous rakabdars (chefs) created pulaos that became works of art. Another distinction between pulaos and biryanis is that pulaos are always simpler and milder as compared to biryanis.

Awadh was the birthplace of the finest biryanis in India. Awadhi biryanis had the meat and the rice prepared separately, which was eventually combined together. The meat would be marinated with yoghurt and aromatic spices, ground onions and ginger and garlic pastes which would be added to the parboiled rice. Alternate layers of meat and rice would then be placed in a heavy-bottomed pot and sealed tightly with kneaded dough and finally simmered or slowly cooked for hours for all the flavours to be infused.

According to legend, in 1784 during a terrible famine, Nawab Asaf ud Daula gave succour to his people by feeding them rice and meat that was cooked in giant pots which were then sealed with dough and allowed to simmer and cook. Thus was born the dum pukht style of cooking. This has been Lucknow's best contribution to Indian cuisine.

MUTTON BIRYANI

SERVES: 8–10   PREPARATION TIME: 1½ HOURS

INGREDIENTS

Basmati rice (long-grained and old)	500 gms
Mutton puth ka gosht (short loin chops)	500 gms
Onions	3 medium, finely chopped
Tomatoes	3 medium, finely chopped
Dahi (yoghurt)	2 cups
Adhrak-lahsun (ginger-garlic) paste	3 tbsp
Laal mirch (red chilli) powder	1½ tsp
Badaam (almonds)	8–10, blanched and peeled
Magaz (watermelon and musk melon) seeds	2 tbsp
Shahi jeera (black cumin) seeds	1 tsp
Meat masala	1 tbsp
Kaali mirch (whole black peppercorns)	1 tsp
Javitri (mace)	3–4 flakes
Jaiphal (nutmeg)	1 small piece
Badi elaichi (black cardamom)	3 pods, whole
Chakr phool (star anise)	5 pieces
Laung (cloves)	1 tsp
Tejpatta (bay leaf)	3 small leaves
Dalchini (cinnamon) stick	1-inch piece
Hari elaichi (green cardamoms)	4 pods
Kewra (screw pine) water	2 tbsp
Kesar (saffron)	½ tsp
Chandi ka varq (silver leaf)	3-4 leaves
Milk	4 tbsp, warmed
Desi ghee	4 tbsp
Sunflower oil	4 tbsp, for frying the meat
Salt	1 tbsp

METHOD

Wash the mutton and drain the water. Add the finely chopped onions
and tomatoes, yoghurt, 1 tablespoon of oil and mix all the ingredients

together except almonds. Marinate for 1 hour.

Wash and soak the rice in lots of water for 45 minutes. The water should completely cover the rice. After 45 minutes drain the water.

Boil 1 litre of water with the cinnamon, black pepper, cloves, bay leaf, black cardamom, star anise and 1 tablespoon of salt. Once the water starts to boil, add the rice. After one boil, reduce the flame and cook for 10 minutes. After it is half done, drain the water and transfer the rice to a wide pan to let it air out. When the rice is well spread out, it does not stick together.

In a kadhai (Indian wok), heat the oil and add the marinated meat to roast. Cook the mutton until it becomes a little tender and the oil rises to the surface.

Mix the mace and the saffron in lukewarm milk. Add this mixture to half the quantity (250 grams) of the rice. Then mix together both the quantities of rice.

In a heavy-bottomed pateela, first add the rice at the bottom and then add the roasted, cooked meat, kewra water and desi ghee and cover it with a heavy lid. Seal it with kneaded dough. On a low flame, take a large pan and place the heavy-bottomed pateela filled with rice on top of the pan. Simmer for about 40 minutes.

Open the lid and garnish with blanched almonds. Decorate with silver leaves. Serve hot with Kachoomber Salad, Burhani Raita (See page 126 under Raitas) and Mint Chutney (See page 206 under Chutneys)

KACHOOMBER SALAD/INDIAN SALAD
(CUCUMBER SALAD)

SERVES: 4   PREPARATION TIME: 15 MIN

INGREDIENTS

White onions	2 medium, finely chopped
Tomatoes	3 large, finely cut and pulp removed
Kheera (cucumber)	3 small, peeled and finely chopped
Pudina (mint) leaves	1 tbsp, finely chopped

Hara dhania (coriander) leaves	½ cup, finely chopped
Hari mirch (green chilli)	3 deseeded and finely chopped
Lime juice	3 tbsp
Shahi jeera (black cumin) seeds	½ tsp
Kaali mirch (black pepper)	¼ tsp
Laal mirch (red chilli) powder	1 tsp
Kaala namak (rock salt)	1 tsp

METHOD

Freshly chop all the ingredients, just prior to serving. In a medium-sized glass bowl, mix all the ingredients together.

This Indian salad is a good accompaniment to most Lucknowi meals, but is an essential side dish with all the biryanis and pulaos.

KATHAL KI BIRYANI
(JACKFRUIT BIRYANI)

SERVES: 8–10   PREPARATION TIME: 1½ HOURS

INGREDIENTS

Kachha kathal (raw jackfruit)	1 kg, cut into 1½-inch squares
Basmati rice (long-grained and old)	½ kg, soaked in water for 45 minutes
Onions	3 medium, finely chopped
Tomatoes	3 medium, finely chopped
Hara dhania (coriander)	12 leaves, finely chopped
Dahi (yoghurt)	½ cup
Adhrak-lahsun (ginger-garlic) paste	4 tbsp
Dhania (coriander) powder	1 tsp
Garam masala (ground spices)	1 tbsp
Kaali mirch (whole black peppercorns)	1 tsp
Badaam (almonds)	8–10, blanched and skin peeled
Magaz (watermelon and musk melon) seeds	2 tbsp
Shahi jeera (black cumin) seeds	1 tsp
Javitri (mace)	3–4 flakes
Jaiphal (nutmeg)	1 small piece

Badi elaichi (black cardamom)	3 pods, whole
Chakr phool (star anise)	5 pieces
Laung (cloves)	1 tsp
Tejpatta (bay leaf)	3 small leaves
Dalchini (cinnamon) stick	1-inch piece
Hari elaichi (green cardamoms)	4 pods
Kewra (screw pine) water	2 tbsp
Kesar (saffron)	½ tsp
Chandi ka varq (silver leaf)	3-4 leaves
Milk	4 tbsp, warmed
Desi ghee	4 tbsp
Mustard oil	2 cups
Salt	2 tsp

METHOD

In a kadhai (Indian wok), heat mustard oil till it starts to smoke. Then deep-fry the jackfruit until it turns golden brown. Remove the jackfruit with a perforated spoon and place on a paper towel to absorb the excess oil.

In the same kadhai, with the remaining oil, fry the finely chopped onions until browned. Add the ginger and garlic paste and cook for a minute. Put in the chopped tomatoes, add all the ingredients, except the almonds to this mixture and roast well until the oil rises to the surface. Then add the yoghurt and cook further for 5 minutes, until the yoghurt blends in with all the spices.

On a high flame, add the jackfruit to this mixture and cook for 5 minutes. Add the finely chopped coriander leaves and the jackfruit is ready. Keep aside.

Add the saffron to the milk. As it releases the aroma pour over the rice the same way as in Mutton Biryani (see page 133). Then, in a heavy-bottomed pateela, first add the rice at the bottom and then add the fried jackfruit, rose water and desi ghee and cover it with a heavy lid. Seal it with kneaded dough.

On a slow flame, take a large pan and place the heavy-bottomed pateela filled with rice on top of the pan. Simmer for about 40 minutes. Open the lid and garnish with blanched almonds. Decorate with silver leaves. Serve hot with Kachoomber Salad (see page 134) and Burhani Raita (see page 126).

ZAFFRANI PULAO
(CHICKEN PULAO FLAVOURED WITH SAFFRON)

SERVES: 8   PREPARATION TIME: 1 HOUR

INGREDIENTS

Basmati rice (long-grained and old)	500 gms, soaked in water for 45 minutes
Chicken	1 kg, cut into 12 pieces
Dahi (yoghurt)	3 cups
Onions	½ cup
Adhrak (ginger) paste	3 tbsp
Lahsun (garlic) paste	3 tbsp
Laal mirch (red chilli) powder	2 tsp
Kesar (saffron)	7–8 strands, soaked in 1 tsp of warmed milk
Tejpatta (bay leaves)	2 leaves
Hari elaichi (green cardamom)	10 pods
Laung (clove)	10 cloves
Badi elaichi (black cardamom)	2 pods
Dalchini (cinnamon)	4 sticks, 1-inch long
Javitri (mace)	1 tsp
Shahi jeera (black cumin seeds)	3 tsp
Butter/desi ghee	¾ cup (unsalted)
Pudina (mint leaves)	2 tbsp, finely chopped
Hara dhania (coriander)	20 leaves, finely chopped
Cream	2½ tbsp
Water	4 litres
Lime juice	2 tsp
Almonds	15 blanched, peeled and halved
Salt	1 tbsp or to taste

METHOD
In a bowl, whisk the yoghurt and divide it into two equal portions.

Mix the saffron and the cream together. Add one portion of the yoghurt to this mixture. Then add the finely chopped mint and green coriander leaves.

In a saucepan, bring the water to a boil and add 1 bay leaf, 2 cloves and 2 green cardamoms. Then add the drained rice and salt. Boil for a couple of minutes until the rice is half cooked. Drain the rice along with the whole spices and keep aside.

On a medium flame, heat the butter/ghee in a pan and sauté the remaining whole spices, black cumin seeds and onions until they turn golden brown. Add the ginger and garlic pastes and red chilli powder. Stir for 30 seconds. Then add the chicken and salt according to taste and cook further for 5 minutes.

To the chicken add approximately 1 cup of water add the rest of the yoghurt, stir and bring to a boil. Lower the flame and let it simmer until the chicken is almost done. Stir in the lime juice.

In a pateela, spread half the chicken mixture and sprinkle half the saffron-yoghurt mixture over it. Now layer half of the parboiled rice over it. Repeat the same process for the remaining half. Cover with a moist cloth and seal the dish with kneaded dough. Let it dum cook, on medium flame for 30 minutes. Remove and serve hot, garnished with fried almond halves.

YAKHNI PULAO
(PULAO COOKED WITH MUTTON BROTH)

SERVES: 8   PREPARATION TIME: 1 HOUR

INGREDIENTS

Mutton	1 kg, neck, back, chest and shoulder cuts with fat
Basmati rice (long-grained and old)	1 kg, soaked for 45 minutes
Onions	3 large, 2 finely chopped and 1 thinly sliced
Tomatoes	3 medium, finely chopped
Dahi (yoghurt)	1 cup

Adhrak (ginger) paste	1 tbsp
Lahsun (garlic) paste	1 tbsp
Badi elaichi (black cardamom)	5 pods
Laung (cloves)	15 cloves
Hari elaichi (green cardamom)	5 pods
Dalchini (cinnamon)	2 sticks, 1-inch long
Kaali mirch (black pepper)	15 peppercorns
Laal mirch (red chilli) powder	1 tsp
Kewra (screw pine) water	2 tbsp
Ghee	6 tbsp
Salt	2 tbsp

METHOD

In a kadhai, melt 3 tablespoons of ghee and add 2 finely chopped onions. Cook until they turn light brown. Add the ginger and garlic pastes, red chilli powder, tomatoes and all the whole spices with 1 tablespoon salt along with the yoghurt. Then add the mutton pieces and cook for 15 minutes.

No water is to be added as the meat will cook in the yoghurt. The ghee will rise to the surface and the meat will be half done.

In a pateela, add the remaining 3 tablespoons of ghee and fry the sliced onion until it turns golden brown. Then add 2 litres of water to the onion. Add all the whole spices with 1 tablespoon of salt. Boil this water for 5 minutes to get the aroma from the spices. To this, add the half-done meat and the soaked rice. On a high flame, bring to a boil, then reduce the flame and add the screw pine water.

Then, cover the pan with a tight-fitting lid and seal it with kneaded dough and place a heavy stone or grindstone over the lid to prevent the steam from escaping. The dum process has started. Cook for 10 minutes. Open the lid and serve hot.

NOORMEHALI PULAO

SERVES: 8   PREPARATION TIME: 1 HOUR

INGREDIENTS

Basmati rice (long-grained and old)	½ kg, soaked in water for 45 minutes
Paneer (cottage cheese)	1 cup, grated
Water/Chicken stock	2 cups
Thick cream	2 tbsp
Onion	½ cup, finely chopped
White onion	1 small
Besan (gram flour)	3 tbsp
Hari mirch (green chilli)	2 deseeded and finely chopped
Hara dhania (coriander leaves)	3 tbsp, finely chopped
Adhrak (ginger) paste	2 tsp
Tejpatta (bay leaf)	2 leaves
Dalchini (cinnamon)	3 sticks, 1-inch long
Laung (clove)	6 cloves
Hari elaichi (green cardamom)	8 pods
Sabut kaali mirch (black peppercorns)	10 peppercorns
Shahi jeera (black cumin) seeds	1 tsp
Javitri (mace) powder	1 tsp
Garam masala (ground spices)	3 tsp
Kesar (saffron)	4–5 strands, soaked in 1 tsp warmed milk
Chandi ka varq (silver leaves)	4 leaves
Desi ghee	4 tbsp
Vegetable oil	2 cups, for frying
Cornflour	2 tbsp
Salt	1 tbsp or to taste

METHOD

This pulao can be made with paneer koftas or minced meat koftas.

Heat the desi ghee in a heavy-bottomed pan and add the bay leaves, cinnamon sticks, cloves, black cumin seeds, green cardamoms and black peppercorns. On a medium flame, sauté the spices until they begin to sputter. Then add the chopped onions with the mace powder and sauté. Add the ginger paste and 1 teaspoon garam masala and cook for 30–40 seconds.

On a medium flame, add the soaked rice and cook for 4–5 minutes stirring occasionally. Then add the water or the chicken stock, Bring this mixture to a boil. Add the salt and lower the flame. Cover the pan and continue to cook the rice until the liquid has been absorbed. Ensure that the rice is not overcooked.

Mix the paneer (see page 216 under Home-made and Organic) with 2 tablespoons of thick cream, besan, white onion, 2 green chillies, freshly chopped coriander leaves and season it with 2 teaspoons of garam masala and 1 teaspoon of salt. Divide this mixture into two portions. Mix one portion with the saffron dissolved in milk and keep the second portion without the saffron colour.

Separately, make small kofta-sized balls from the two mixtures. Then roll them in 2 tablespoons of cornflour to maintain their shape while frying. Deep-fry the paneer koftas in hot oil. These koftas are called Noormehals.

Transfer the pulao to a large serving platter. Gild the Noormehali koftas with the chandi ka varq (silver leaves) and place them on top of the pulao. Serve hot.

Note: For the non-vegetarian version, prepare the pulao as above with the minced meat koftas (as on page 88 under Lucknowi Mutton).

SUBZION KI TEHRI
(VEGETABLE PULAO)

SERVES: 8   PREPARATION TIME: 1 HOUR

INGREDIENTS

Basmati rice   2 cups, washed, soaked and drained

For the potli (bouquet garni)
The following spices are to be pounded in a mortar and pestle and tied in a muslin cloth.

Kaali mirch (black peppercorns)	12 peppercorns
Saunf (fennel) seeds	2 tsp
Hari elaichi (green cardamom)	5 pods
Badi elaichi (black cardamom)	4 pods
Laung (cloves)	4 cloves
Tejpatta (bay leaves)	2 leaves
Dalchini (cinnamon)	1-inch stick

For the vegetables

Baby potatoes	6 small and even-sized, peeled
Phool gobi (cauliflower)	100 gms, florets cut into halves
Gajar (carrots)	100 gms, coarsely chopped
Faras beans (French beans)	100 gms, coarsely chopped
Hara mattar (green peas)	50 gms
White baby onions	6 small
Onion	1 medium, thinly sliced
Hari mirch (green chilli)	4, deseeded and slit
Laal mirch (red chilli) powder	1 tsp
Haldi (turmeric) powder	2 tbsp
Water	4 cups
Lime juice	1 tbsp
Desi ghee	4 tbsp
Salt	1 tbsp

METHOD

Soak the rice for 45 minutes in 2 litres of water. Drain the water and keep the rice aside.

In 4 cups of boiling water, add the bouquet garni, cover and simmer for 5 minutes. Remove the potli and squeeze the muslin cloth, you will notice the water turning brown with the fragrance and the colour of the spices. Remove the bouquet garni.

In a large heavy-bottomed pan, heat the desi ghee, sauté the thinly sliced onions and add the fragrant spiced water to the onions. When the water comes to a boil, add all the chopped vegetables including the whole baby onions and the whole baby potatoes. Add the soaked rice. Then add the turmeric, red chilli powder and salt. Once it comes to a boil, reduce the flame and cover it with a lid. Cook for 5–7 minutes with the green chillies.

Finally, squeeze the lime juice evenly on top of the Tehri. Serve hot with Burhani Raita (see page 126 and Kachoomber Salad (see page 134).

Rotis and Parathas

As much as the province of Awadh was famous for its varied kebabs, it also excelled in breads. Muslims initially ate leavened bread baked in underground clay ovens. They watched the Hindus fry their unleavened bread, such as puris, in ghee. From this, Muslim bakers were inspired to add ghee to their bread and griddles. And thus, the invention of the paratha.

Sheermals, which originated in Lucknow, are the pride of Awadh. This invention of the late nineteenth century was attributed to a non-Lucknowi vendor named Mahamadu. Sheermal means 'washed with milk' in Persian. This unleavened bread became so popular that no celebration or function would be considered complete without it. It is a speciality in Lucknow even today and is very different from the sheermals served in Meerut or New Delhi, according to Parveen Talha, chronicler of Lucknow's social history and cuisine.

Another variation of sheermal is the baqarkhani which is an improved version of the paratha. Baqarkhanis are an extravagant kind of bread, suited to a rich man's palate.

Warqi Parathas, on the other hand, are a meal in themselves. This multilayered flaky and fried form of bread from Awadh is an ideal accompaniment with all Lucknowi curries and kebabs and a gourmet's delight.

METHI KI ROTI

MAKES: 36 SMALL ROTIS   PREPARATION TIME: 45 MINUTES

INGREDIENTS

Atta (wheat flour)	500 gms
Maida (refined flour)	500 gms
Methi (fenugreek) leaves	500 gms
Hari mirch (green chilli)	5 pieces
Dhania (coriander) powder	1 tsp
Garam masala (ground spices)	½ tsp
Onion	1 large, finely chopped
Haldi (turmeric) powder	½ tsp
Ajwain (caraway) seeds	1 tsp
Sunflower oil	2 tbsp
Milk	200 ml
Salt	1 tbsp or to taste

METHOD

Mix all the above ingredients to form a smooth dough and keep it in a cool place, wrapped in a muslin cloth, for approximately one hour.

Cook the rotis, smearing lightly with desi ghee.

LACHHA PARATHA

MAKES: 16   PREPARATION TIME: 30 MINUTES

INGREDIENTS

Atta (wholewheat flour)	250 gms
Maida (refined flour)	250 gms
Milk	100 ml
Desi ghee/Oil	4 tbsp/2 tbsp
Salt	1 tsp or to taste

METHOD

Knead the atta and maida with water. Add water slowly along with a little desi ghee (or oil) and milk and knead into a smooth dough. Keep aside for an hour. Roll into thin rotis, 8 inches in diameter. Sprinkle dry flour on the rotis while rolling.

Liberally apply the ghee (or oil) on the roti. Again lightly sprinkle some dry flour over the roti. From one end start pleating it in like a paper fan until you reach the other end. Twist this pleated dough. Coil it into a tight circle with the edges joined together.

Using a rolling pin, start rolling the dough into parathas. Season the griddle (tawa) with a teaspoon of oil and place the paratha on the hot tawa. Fry the paratha in the oil, flipping it until both sides are cooked and browned.

Finally, tap the hot paratha hard with your palms a couple of times. This is done to loosen the layers. Generously smear the paratha with desi ghee. Lachha Paratha is ready. Serve hot.

ULTEY TAWE KI ROTI
(UNLEAVENED BREAD COOKED ON AN INVERTED GRIDDLE)

MAKES: 6–8   PREPARATION TIME: 30 MINUTES

INGREDIENTS

Maida (refined flour)	250 gms
Kaju (cashew nut) paste	3 tbsp
Castor sugar	1½ tbsp
Milk	1½ cups
Baking powder	1 tsp
Desi ghee	4 tbsp
Salt	to taste

METHOD

In a bowl, sieve together the flour and the salt. Make a well in the centre. In a separate bowl, mix together the cashew paste, sugar, milk and baking powder. Pour this mixture in the centre of the flour and knead it into a smooth dough.

Divide the dough into 8 equal portions and place the balls on a lightly floured paraath (large high-hipped flat platter). Flatten each dough ball between your palms. Then with a rolling pin, roll them into round discs (rotis). Apply 1 teaspoon of melted ghee evenly on each roti and sprinkle dry flour over it.

Then with a knife make a cut from the centre towards the circumference of the dough. From here pick the loose end and start rolling it inwards to form a conical shape. Above the base make spiral movements to compress the cone into a ball. Keep aside for 30–40 minutes. Remove and on a lightly floured surface press the ball and flatten with a rolling pin into an 8-inch roti.

Place the roti on a preheated ulta tawa (inverted griddle), turn it once, and apply ghee. Again press the roti with a dry cloth from all sides until it turns light brown. Apply ghee and remove. Repeat the same process with the rest of the rotis. Serve hot.

WARQI PARATHA

MAKES: 8–10   PREPARATION TIME: 1½ HOURS

INGREDIENTS

Atta (flour)	500 gms
Milk	1 cup
Sugar	2½ tsp
Khus (vetiver) water	2 drops
Desi ghee	200 gms
Salt	to taste

METHOD

In a paraath (large high-hipped flat platter), sieve the flour and the salt. In a separate bowl dissolve the sugar in warm milk, add the vetiver and stir. Make a depression in the sieved flour, pour the milk and half a cup of water into it and mix gradually. When fully mixed, knead it into a dough and cover it with a moist cloth. Keep aside for 30 minutes.

Add two-thirds of the melted ghee gradually to the dough to make it soft. Cover and keep aside for 15 minutes.

Place the dough on a lightly floured paraath and with a rolling pin flatten it into a rectangular shape. Then apply ¼ of the remaining ghee evenly over the rolled out dough, dust it with flour and fold one end over the other to form three folds. Cover and refrigerate the dough for 10 minutes. Repeat this process thrice.

Remove the dough from the refrigerator and place it on the floured paraath, flatten into a rectangle (approximately ⅛ of an inch thick) and make 5-inch diameter rotis (discs). Then make three evenly spaced criss-cross incisions (approximately ½ an inch) on the surface of each roti. Place the rotis on individual sheets of butter paper and refrigerate until they are ready to be served (the longer you refrigerate the rotis the more distinct the warq or flakes become, but not for more than 8–10 hours).

On a heated tawa, shallow-fry both sides over a low flame until light golden in colour. Remove and serve immediately.

BAQARKHANI

MAKES: 8   PREPARATION TIME: 1½ HOURS

INGREDIENTS

Maida (refined flour)	4 cups
Milk	1 cup
Yeast	½ small block, fresh
Baking powder	1 tsp
Sugar	5 tsp
Desi ghee	2/3 cup
Badaam (almonds)	3 tbsp, blanched, skinned and cut into slivers
Khus (vetiver) water	2 drops
Hari elaichi (green cardamom)	4 tsp, powdered
Sunflower seeds	1 tbsp, soaked in water
Flour	to dust
Salt	1 tsp

METHOD

Sieve the flour with the baking powder and salt into a paraath. Dissolve the sugar in warm milk, add vetiver and stir.

Dissolve the yeast in ½ a cup of warm water. Make a depression in the sieved flour, pour the milk and the dissolved yeast in it and mix gradually. When fully mixed, knead the flour into dough. Cover with a moist cloth and keep aside for 15 minutes.

Add the melted ghee gradually to the dough to make it soft. Then add the almonds, green cardamom powder and sunflower seed and knead again. Cover and keep in a warm place for 30 minutes to allow the dough to rise.

Divide into 12 equal-sized portions and shape them into balls, sprinkled with dry flour. Cover and keep aside for 10 minutes. Place the dough balls on a lightly floured paraath and flatten each ball with a rolling pin into round rotis (discs) of approximately 7-inch diameter. Prick the entire surface with a fork.

Pre-heat the oven to 350°F/180°C. Arrange the rotis on a pre-greased baking tray and bake in the oven for 7–8 minutes. Remove from the oven and lightly baste with ghee. The Baqarkhani is ready. Serve hot.

SHEERMAL

MAKES: 6–8   PREPARATION TIME: 1 HOUR

INGREDIENTS

Maida (refined flour)	3 cups
Milk	1 cup
Sugar	1½ tsp
Khus (vetiver) water	2 drops
Desi ghee	¾ cup, melted
Flour	to dust
Kesar (saffron)	4–5 strands, soaked well in 2 tbsp warm milk
Salt	1 tsp or to taste

METHOD

In a paraath, mix together the flour, the melted ghee, sugar and salt. Gradually add the milk, a little at a time and rub in the ghee, kneading the flour into a smooth dough. Cover and keep aside for 2 hours. Knead again and keep it aside for 2 more hours.

Divide this soft dough into equal-sized portions and shape it into balls. Then with the help of a rolling pin, roll the dough into 6-inch round discs (rotis), about ¼-inch thick and prick the entire roti with a fork.

On a heated tawa, shallow-fry the roti over a low flame until it turns brown on both sides. Smear the sheermal, one at a time, with the soaked saffron milk and khus water and then cook for a minute. Serve hot, basted with ghee.

Meetha

When it comes to meetha, Lucknowi preparations perhaps outshine those from many other regions in the country in terms of taste and delicacy.

A famous and unique Lucknow speciality is Nimish, a beautiful and delicate frothy dessert which can be made only during the cold winter months. The basic preparation of Nimish is when milk is poured into large flat pans and left in the open before dawn. When the early morning dew falls on the milk, it creates a froth which is as light as air. This is continuously collected and later mixed in with cream and other condiments. It is a laborious and painstaking process. A version of Nimish which can be made at home is included in this cookbook as this meetha is a signature dessert of Lucknow. The Nimish of Lucknow is very different from the Daulat ki Chaat available in Delhi.

Muzaafar is a sweet delicacy made out of fine vermicelli. This particular recipe was given to me by my school friend Nilofer Ali, née Qureshi. In school, Nilofer was a champion sportswoman who had only wielded a bat and never a karhchi (ladle), as she had never been inside a kitchen. Now she is a consummate cook.

Sheer Korma or Khurma is derived from sheer (milk) and khurma (dates) combined with vermicelli and dry fruit. It is a mouthwatering and celebrated dessert during Ramadan and Eid.

Shahi Tukra means 'royal pieces' of bread. According to legend, this baadshahi dessert was invented by the old khansamas who disliked throwing away leftover or day-old bread. So, instead, they made the best use of it by converting it into a royal dessert. The bread is deep-fried in ghee and then soaked in sweetened creamy milk, flavoured with saffron and pistachios and generously decorated with gold and silver leaves (varq). It was so popular among the Mughals that they enjoyed this dessert even for breakfast during the month of Ramadan.

The Lucknow nobility followed suit.

Other favourite meethas of Lucknow are Badaam ki Kheer, a sweet creamy dessert made with pounded almonds and rice. Rabarhi is a popular milk pudding garnished with pistachios that tastes delicious with jalebis. Phirni is a simple rice pudding prepared in almost every house.

Halwa or halva, a word derived from Arabic, means 'sweet or sweetness', and is a grain or lentil-based dessert made with ghee and sugar. It was introduced to Indians through the trade route from the Middle East. In Lucknow, halwas were made with various combinations of lentil, flour, semolina, fresh fruit, carrots, etc. The cheaply available chana ki dal (chickpea lentil) was roasted and ground to flour to make the perfect Chane ki Dal ka Halwa, a rich dessert.

My friend Zakia Zaheer makes, perhaps, the best Kali Gajar (black carrot) ka Halwa. She willingly shared the recipe of this seasonal and favourite dessert, which otherwise can only be bought from the Chowk in Lucknow.

My mother's meetha recipes like Steamed Yoghurt, which is blended yoghurt combined with condensed milk, is similar in taste to a delicious cheesecake. Her Aam Malai, made with the purée of luscious ripe mangoes, is very simple and loved by everyone.

The kulfi made in our house is, perhaps, the best home-made kulfi. This recipe was devised by my husband, Rome, and is always available in our refrigerator, be it summer or winter. This simple recipe is light, made without khoya and served without faluda.

MUZAAFAR
(SWEET VERMICELLI)

SERVES: 10–12   PREPARATION TIME: 1 HOUR

INGREDIENTS

Sewian (fine vermicelli)	250 gms
Desi ghee	250 gms
Milk	2 cups
Sugar	2½ cups
Kewra (screw pine) water	2–3 drops
Khoya (whole milk fudge)	250 gms, crumbled or grated
Badaam (almonds)	20 blanched and slivered
Chandi ka varq (silver leaf)	2 leaves

METHOD

Heat the ghee in a kadhai. Fry the vermicelli in 5 to 6 batches until light brown (if you are using pre-roasted vermicelli, fry each batch for 1–2 minutes). Remove and drain the vermicelli on an absorbent kitchen paper towel.

Boil the milk in a saucepan. Remove from the stove and add the fried vermicelli. Press gently with a spoon so that all the vermicelli is moistened. Cover and leave to soak for 10 minutes.

Melt the sugar in a separate pan with ½ a cup of water, stirring on gentle heat until the sugar dissolves completely. Then boil rapidly for one minute. Pour the sugar syrup on the vermicelli and milk mixture and return the pan on a low flame. Cover and cook for 15–20 undisturbed minutes, or until the liquid has been absorbed. Each strand of vermicelli should be separate. Add screw pine essence and whole milk fudge and gently turn with a fork to mix it in. Serve chilled in a glass dish, garnished with slivered almonds and chandi ka varq.

NIMISH
(LUCKNOW SOUFFLÉ)

SERVES: 4   PREPARATION TIME: 2–2½ HOURS

INGREDIENTS

Full-cream milk	8 cups, unboiled
Cream	2 cups
Cream of tartar	1 tsp
Castor sugar	1 cup
Gulab jal (rose water)	1 tsp
Pista (pistachios)	2 tbsp, finely sliced

METHOD

Combine the milk, cream and the cream of tartar in a large bowl and refrigerate overnight.

Next morning stir in 4 teaspoons of castor sugar and 1 teaspoon of rose water and whisk the mixture, using a rotary or electric beater at a high speed. Using a large tea strainer, collect the foam that forms and transfer it to a large tray. Keep the tray tilted so that the foam stays on one side while the milk collects on the lower side.

When the tray is fairly full, spoon the foam into small glass ramekins, sprinkling a little castor sugar between each layer and on top of it. The foam will condense a little during this operation. What looks like four bowlfuls in the tray will make only two bowls.

Pour the milk collected in the tray back into the bowl and continue beating and collecting the foam until all the milk is finished. This whole process will take approximately 2 to 2½ hours. Sprinkle pistachios on top of each bowl of foam. Refrigerate until you serve.

SHEER KORMA
(VERMICELLI PUDDING)

SERVES: 8   PREPARATION TIME: 30 MINUTES

INGREDIENTS

Sewian (fine vermicelli)	100 gms
Milk	2½ cups
Khajur (dried dates)	2–3 soaked in water and finely slivered
Sugar	4 tbsp
Raisins	1 tsp
Kesar (saffron)	3–4 strands
Gulab ka itr (rose essence)	a few drops
Pista (pistachios)	2 tsp, sliced, for garnish
Badaam (almonds)	10 soaked in water, peeled and slivered, to garnish

METHOD

Boil the vermicelli on a dry griddle (tawa) to a pale gold. Set aside to cool. Boil the milk and add the vermicelli. Cook on a low flame for 15 minutes. Add the slivered dates, sugar and raisins and cook for 2 minutes.

Soak the saffron in a little milk or water and add it to this mixture. Let it simmer for about 10 minutes, stirring all the time.

Sheer Korma may be served hot or cold. Garnish with slivered almonds, sliced pistachios and sprinkle with rose essence. For special occasions, chandi ka varq (silver leaf) may be used before garnishing with the almonds and pistachios.

STEAMED YOGHURT

SERVES: 8   PREPARATION TIME: 10 MINUTES

                                    COOKING TIME: 1 TO 1½ HOURS

INGREDIENTS

Dahi (yoghurt)	2 cups / ½ kg
Condensed milk	1 tin
Grated lime or orange rind	1 tsp

METHOD

Blend the yoghurt and condensed milk until smooth. Add the grated
rind. Pour into an oven-proof dish and cover with its lid. Bake at a low
heat of 100°C or steam for 20 minutes in a double boiler. Then test by
inserting a knife in the centre. It should come out clean.

This dessert tastes like cheesecake. There are several options for
garnishing this dessert: guava jelly (see page 178), stewed fruit (see page
175) or home-made marmalades of various citrus fruit.

SHAHI TUKRA
(INDIAN BREAD PUDDING)

SERVES: 8   PREPARATION TIME: 15 MINUTES

                                    COOKING TIME: 15 MINUTES

INGREDIENTS

Bread loaf (one day old)	12–16 slices, crusts removed
Milk	2 cups
Khoya (whole milk fudge)	1 cup, crushed
Sugar	1 cup
Water	½ cup
Desi ghee	1 cup
Gulab jal (rose water)	4–5 drops
Badaam (almond) paste	1 tbsp
Kishmish (raisins)	10 raisins, soaked

Pista (pistachios)	¼ cup, slivered
Badaam (almonds)	¼ cup, slivered
Kesar (saffron)	½ tsp (liquefied) and a pinch for garnishing
Chandi ka varq (silver leaf)	for garnishing

METHOD

Cut the slices of bread neatly into triangular or rectangular pieces. Fry them in ghee on a low flame to a golden colour. Coat them with the almond paste.

Mix the sugar and water to make sugar syrup of a single thread consistency. Keep it on a low flame. Add the saffron and mix well. Dip each slice of bread into the hot syrup, remove and keep on a tray.

Reduce the milk to half by boiling it. Add the crushed khoya (see page 218 under Home-made and Organic) and mix it in well.

On a flat pan, spread the bread slices in a single layer. Pour half the milk mixture over them. Then sprinkle the nuts. Pour the remaining milk mixture and sugar syrup over this and cook the slices until almost all the liquid is absorbed. Take it off the flame and add the pinch of saffron and essence (rose water) over it. Garnish with the slivered almonds, pistachios and silver leaf (chandi ka varq).

PHIRNI
(RICE PUDDING)

This is a popular dessert, traditionally set in shikoras (small earthenware bowls) and flavoured with saffron and crushed cardamom seeds.

SERVES: 8   PREPARATION TIME: 1½ HOURS

INGREDIENTS

Rice (basmati or fine old)	¼ cup
Milk	1 litre
Sugar	1¼ cup
Kewra (screw pine) water	1 tbsp
Gulab jal (rose water)	2 drops

Kesar (saffron)	1 tsp
Hari elaichi (green cardamom)	1 tsp, freshly crushed pods
Chandi ka varq (silver leaf)	2 leaves
Rose petals	for garnishing
Almonds or pistachios	4 tsp, slivered

METHOD

Wash the rice and soak it in water for an hour. Drain and pound the rice. Add a little milk to the pounded rice to make a fine paste.

Boil the rest of the milk with crushed green cardamom pods and add the rice paste to it. Stir continuously so that lumps do not form. When the mixture becomes thick and creamy, add sugar and cook for 5 minutes. Add both the essences and cover. Take off the fire, add the saffron and stir continuously while it cools.

Transfer into an earthenware dish (shikoras) or into individual glass bowls/ramekins or into a large glass dish. Leave to set and cool in the fridge for half an hour. Before serving, decorate with silver leaf, rose petals and slivered nuts (almonds or pistachios). Phirni can also be prepared a day before it is required to be served. It keeps well in the fridge.

Note: If using the shikoras, rinse in running water and then immerse in a pot full of water for 25 minutes. Remove and pat dry before using them.

BADAAM KI KHEER
(ALMOND PUDDING)

SERVES: 8   PREPARATION TIME: 1 HOUR

INGREDIENTS

Full-cream milk	2 litres
Badaam (almonds)	1 cup, pounded
Whipped cream	1 cup
Rice	2 tbsp, finely pounded
Sugar	1½ cups

Chandi ka varq (silver leaf)	2–3 leaves
Almonds (for garnishing)	10–12 soaked, peeled and slivered

METHOD

Boil the milk well, stirring continuously without allowing any skin to form. While stirring, add the pounded rice and the whipped cream. When this mixture becomes rich and creamy, add the pounded almonds and sugar. Cook further until the mixture thickens and then take off the fire.

Pour into a large glass bowl or individual glass dessert bowls to set. Decorate with silver leaf (chandi ka varq) and slivered almonds. Serve chilled.

KALI GAJAR KA HALWA
(BLACK CARROT HALWA)

This is a Lucknow speciality. Kali Gajar (black carrots) are available only in the winter season and this halwa can only be bought in the Chowk in Lucknow.

SERVES: 8   PREPARATION TIME: 1 HOUR

INGREDIENTS

Kali gajar	1 kg
Desi ghee	250 gms
Full-cream milk	1 kg
Khoya (whole milk fudge)	250 gms
Sugar	250 gms
Hari elaichi (green cardamom)	½ tsp, pounded pods
Almonds and pistachios	12 each, soaked, peeled and slivered
Khoya, almonds, pistachios and silver leaf	for garnishing

METHOD

Wash, peel and grate the carrots. Boil the milk and let the carrots cook in it until they are tender and the milk is absorbed. Once the milk is absorbed, roast them for 5 minutes. Then add the ghee and further roast. When the ghee separates and the carrots are well roasted, add the sugar.

Roast the khoya separately until it is red and the raw taste disappears. Set aside a little raw khoya for the garnishing. Add the roasted khoya to the halwa. Mix in well. Add the ground cardamom and mix in. Decorate with white khoya pieces, almond and pistachio slivers and silver leaf (chandi ka varq).

AAM MALAI
(MANGO CREAM DESSERT)

SERVES: 8   PREPARATION TIME: 1 HOUR

INGREDIENTS

Mango purée	6 well-ripened mangoes (aamras colour)
Heavy cream	¾ cup and 1 tbsp
Sugar	2 tbsp
Gelatin	1½ tsp powdered or 1½ envelopes unflavoured

METHOD

To the mango purée, add the cream and sugar and mix well. Prepare the gelatin by dissolving it in half a cup of boiling water, stirring continuously until it is fully dissolved. Pour the gelatin into the mango mixture and whisk it briskly. Transfer the mixture into a serving bowl, swirl a tablespoon of cream over the top and refrigerate for 3 to 4 hours, until the mango cream is set. Serve chilled. This can also be set and served in individual glass bowls.

RABARHI
(MILK PUDDING)

SERVES: 12   PREPARATION TIME: 2 HOURS

INGREDIENTS

Milk	3 litres
Sugar	350 gms
Khus (vetiver) water	5 drops
Pistachios	12 nuts, peeled and slivered
Chandi ka varq (silver leaf)	2–3 leaves

METHOD

Pour the milk into a kadhai and bring to a boil. Reduce to a low flame, stirring continuously for 20–25 minutes. Then stir every 5 minutes until the milk is reduced to approximately 4 cups and it has acquired a granular consistency.

Remove from the fire and add the sugar, stirring continuously until the sugar has completely dissolved. Then stir in the vetiver drops. Let it cool. Transfer into a serving dish and garnish with the pistachio slivers. Refrigerate. Before serving, decorate it with silver leaf.

KULFI
(INDIAN ICE CREAM)

SERVES: 8   PREPARATION TIME: 15 MINUTES

INGREDIENTS

Full-cream milk	8 cups/2 litres
Sugar	½ cup/150 gms
Condensed milk	1 tin
Metal kulfi moulds	8 moulds, washed and well-dried
Optional:	
Kewra (screw pine) essence	2–3 drops
Badaam (almonds)	10–12 blanched and slivered

Pistachios	10–12 blanched and slivered
Hari elaichi (green cardamom) seeds	1 tsp
Kesar (saffron)	3–4 strands

METHOD

Boil the milk and sugar in a large heavy-bottomed pan, stirring from time to time until it reduces to approximately half the original quantity and becomes thick and creamy. This will take 30–40 minutes.

If any of the optional items are to be used, add them at this point and cook for 5 minutes.

Let the mixture cool to room temperature. Now, stir in the condensed milk. Spoon the mixture into the kulfi moulds. Tightly cover the moulds and freeze them overnight. To serve, roll the mould in your hands or use wet warm towels to invert the kulfi onto individual dessert plates.

CHANE KI DAL KA HALWA
(LENTIL HALWA)

SERVES: 10   PREPARATION TIME: 1½ HOURS

INGREDIENTS

Chane ki dal (gram lentil)	½ kg, washed in warm water and soaked for 1 hour
Milk/Powdered milk	6 cups (1½ litres)/2 cups (250 gms)
Desi ghee	2½ cups
Sugar	2 cups
Badaam (almonds)	10 soaked in warm water, peeled and slivered
Pista (pistachios)	10 soaked in warm water, peeled and slivered
Hari elaichi (green cardamom) seeds	10 pods, ground with 1 tsp sugar
Akhrot (walnuts)	½ cup, shelled and coarsely chopped
Kishmish (raisins)	15 raisins
Chandi ka varq (silver leaf)	2-3 leaves

Boil the dal until it is tender but remains whole. Then drain and cool. Grind in a blender.

Heat the ghee in a pan, add the cardamom seeds. After a minute add the ground dal. Cook on a low flame, stirring continuously until the dal changes colour to a light brown. Now add the milk, sugar, walnuts and raisins. Continue stirring until the ghee separates from the halwa.

Apply a little ghee to a large shallow serving dish. Transfer the halwa. Decorate the halwa with the almonds and pistachios, then gently place the silver leaves on it. The halwa is ready to be served.

Puddings

Lucknow's favourite comfort pudding has always been Bread Pudding. This was the Anglo-Indian equivalent of Shahi Tukra. But unlike the latter, which was fried in ghee, Bread Pudding was prepared with chunks of bread soaked in milk with dry fruit marinated in brandy, and candied orange peels. It was then baked and served warm from the oven.

Fresh crunchy jalebis (deep-fried yoghurt pretzels) doused in hot sugar syrup, eaten during the rainy season have always been everyone's favourite. My mother's invention was Jalebi Pudding. This is a very simple dessert made with the previous day's jalebis which no one wanted to consume. This frugality and recycling of food into another dish, was I think, part of their generation's refugee psyche.

Her Mango Brûlée Brownie Pudding, Almond Delight, Lemon Tart and Lemon Soufflé are just a few samples of her countless dessert recipes. All are simple to make and yet are divine indulgences. I am always reminded of the limerick:

Each day I ate a cream éclair,
They're hardly more than whipped up air,
They float gently past my lips,
And put two inches on my hips.

In our homes, fruit was eaten fresh but was also stewed and relished with dollops of double cream. My mother's Fruit Salad in Orange Shell is an appealing dessert, both visually and in taste. Other unusual desserts are Guava Cheese and Guava Jelly. The former can be served on its own or with other desserts.

The Everyday Ice Cream in this cookbook, as the name suggests, was made every day in our house. This was set in a separate ice tray for us three siblings, as we ate earlier than our parents. As I was the eldest, I used to be in charge of making three equal portions at dinner time. But unknown to my brother Ashok and my sister Rekha, every day straight after returning from school, I would first scrape off a top layer of the ice cream and relish it on my own. I only confessed this to them on my wedding day. They did not think it was at all amusing and refused to speak to me for much of that evening!

JALEBI PUDDING

SERVES: 8   PREPARATION TIME: 1 HOUR

INGREDIENTS

Jalebi	500 gms
Milk	4 cups
Eggs	3

METHOD

Soak the jalebis in milk for about an hour. Beat the eggs slightly and fold them into the milk and jalebi mixture.

Bake at 350°F/180°C in an oven-proof glass dish, very lightly greased with butter for approximately 30 minutes, until the top is golden brown. Serve hot.

MANGO BRÛLÉE

SERVES: 8   PREPARATION TIME: 10 MINUTES

INGREDIENTS

Aam (mangoes)	4 large, sliced
Eggs	4 lightly beaten
Double cream	1¼ cups, lightly whipped
Brown sugar or demerara	150 gms

METHOD

Fold the eggs into the double cream and pour over the sliced mangoes in a shallow glass serving dish. Cover with the sugar and place under a very hot grill, preheated at 350°F/180°C. Allow the sugar to become dark and bubbly. Refrigerate once it cools. Serve chilled.

BROWNIE PUDDING

SERVES: 8   PREPARATION TIME: 1 HOUR

INGREDIENTS

Refined flour	1 cup, sifted
Baking powder	2 tsp
Cocoa	½ cup, dark cooking cocoa powder
Brown sugar	¾ cup powdered
Walnuts	¾ cup, coarsely chopped
Milk	½ cup
Vanilla essence	1 tsp
Cooking oil	1¼ cups
Hot water	1¾ cups
Salt	1 tsp

METHOD

Sift the refined flour, baking powder and salt into a bowl. To this add the milk, vanilla essence and oil and mix until smooth. Stir in the walnuts and pour into a greased pan (8×8×2 inches).

Mix together the brown sugar and ½ cup of the cooking cocoa. Mix into the batter. Then pour hot water over this batter. Bake at 350°F/180°C for 45 minutes. Serve hot with home-made vanilla ice cream (see page 179).

BREAD PUDDING

SERVES: 6   PREPARATION TIME: 1½ HOURS

INGREDIENTS

White bread	16 slices, sides and crusts removed
Eggs	3 beaten
Cinnamon powder	1 tbsp
Grated nutmeg	½ tsp
Candied orange peel	50 gms, chopped

Orange zest	2 tsp
Lemon zest	1 tsp
Sultanas (raisins)	100 gms
Currants	25 gms
Raisins	25 gms
Brandy	2 tbsp (optional)
Milk	2 cups
Butter	50 gms, melted
Sugar	75 gms

METHOD

Put the sultanas, currants, raisins and the candied orange peel in a bowl. Pour the brandy over the mixture and keep it aside to marinate for 1 hour.

In a large bowl, break the bread into pieces. Then add the milk, mix it in well and keep aside for 30 minutes.

Heat the oven to 350°F/180°C. Mix the melted butter, sugar, cinnamon powder, nutmeg and eggs together. Add this to the bread and milk mixture. Using a fork, beat the mixture well. Then stir in the marinated fruit, with the orange and the lemon zest and any remaining brandy.

Spread the mixture in a greased oven-proof glass dish (approximately 8×6×2 inches). Sprinkle the sugar over it, along with some freshly grated nutmeg. Bake on the middle shelf of the oven for about 1½ hours. Serve the warm pudding straight from the oven.

ALMOND DELIGHT

SERVES: 8   PREPARATION TIME: 1 HOUR

INGREDIENTS

Almonds	½ cup, slivered
Hung yoghurt cheese/cream cheese	1 cup
Single cream	3½ tbsp
Honey	1 tbsp

Castor sugar	3 tbsp
Eggs	3, yolks and egg whites separated
Refined flour	1 tbsp
Butter	1 tbsp
Vanilla essence	1 tsp

METHOD

Pre-heat the oven to 350°F/180°C. Lightly butter an oven-proof glass dish. Mix the butter, half the sugar, the honey, the hung yoghurt cheese/cream cheese, vanilla essence and egg yolks in a processor. Blend well. Add the cream and the flour. Blend again.

Beat the egg whites until stiff but not dry and gradually whisk in the remaining sugar. With a wooden spoon, stir the egg whites into the cream cheese mixture, in two or three batches. Finally, stir in the slivered almonds. Pour the mixture into the dish and bake for 1 hour or until it has set. Turn off the oven and let the pudding cool in the oven. Then refrigerate. Serve chilled.

LEMON TARTS WITH LEMON CURD

SERVES: 6   PREPARATION TIME: 1 HOUR

INGREDIENTS FOR THE TARTS

Maida (All-purpose flour)	1¾ cup
Butter	¾ cup, at room temperature
Sugar	½ cup
Vanilla essence	½ tsp
Salt	¼ tsp

METHOD

In a mixing bowl, combine the butter, sugar, vanilla essence and salt and mix. Then stir the all-purpose flour into this butter mix to make a smooth dough for the tart. Press the dough into a 9-inch tart pan and refrigerate the crust for 30 minutes.

In a heated oven of 350°F/180°C, bake the crust for 15–20 minutes until it turns golden brown.

The Lucknow Cookbook

For tartlets

Follow the same recipe, cut out the dough with a cookie cutter and press these rounds into greased tartlet moulds.

INGREDIENTS FOR LEMON CURD

Limes	3 juiced
Lime rind	1 tsp, grated
Sugar	1 cup
Butter	½ cup
Eggs	2 yolks, room temperature

METHOD

In a bowl, beat the eggs, then beat in the sugar and finally the lime juice. In a saucepan cook this beaten mixture on a low flame until it thickens to custard-like consistency. Then, add the butter and the lime rind. Let it cool. Bottle the lemon curd and refrigerate. Use as and when required.

Then add the lemon curd into the tart and bake for another 20 minutes. Let it cool and serve. The lemon curd can be filled into the tart or the small tartlets. The tart is a pudding and the small tartlets are for coffee and high teas.

LEMON SOUFFLÉ

SERVES: 6   PREPARATION TIME: 1 HOUR

INGREDIENTS

Limes	3, juiced
Lime rind	1 tsp, grated
Eggs	5, yolks and whites separated
Cornflour	3 tbsp, levelled
Castor sugar	1 cup
Milk	3 cups
Gelatin	2 tbsp, dissolved is 4 tbsp of water
Heavy cream	4 tbsp, whipped

METHOD

Grate the rind of the limes (no white pith) and put it into a mixing bowl with the castor sugar. Add 3 egg yolks to the lime rind and sugar along with the cornflour and 1 cup of milk and mix to a smooth creamy consistency. Beat well. Then add the lime juice.

In a saucepan, heat the remaining 2 cups of milk. Take off the flame and then add it to the creamy mixture in the bowl. When it is fully dissolved and mixed evenly with the milk, allow it to cool.

Beat the remaining 2 egg yolks with 2 teaspoons of sugar and stir into the cooked milk. Cook over a double boiler until the mixture has slightly thickened. Take off the flame and let it cool. Then add the dissolved gelatin. When it begins to thicken, fold in the heavy whipped cream and stiffly beaten egg whites. Pour this into a damp soufflé mould and let it chill until it sets. Serve chilled.

FRUIT SALAD IN ORANGE SHELL

SERVES: 8   PREPARATION TIME: 20 MINUTES

INGREDIENTS

Oranges	4 large
Strawberries/any other whole berries	2 cups, chopped
Grapefruit	2 pieces, cut into sections
Lime juice	2 tbsp
Eggs	2 beaten
Honey	½ cup
Cream	¼ cup, whipped
Almonds	12 blanched, peeled and slivered

METHOD

With a sharp fruit knife cut the oranges through their centres, keeping the shells intact. Cut a sliver off each end of the orange, so that it balances on a dessert plate.

Mix the eggs, honey and lime juice and cook on a low flame until it thickens, stirring continuously. Cool and chill.

Carefully remove the sections of the oranges and cut them into large pieces and peel. Remove all the juice and chill.

Beat the cream until stiff and combine with the chilled egg and honey mixture. In a bowl, add all the fruit to the lime juice mixture and fold it into the whipped cream and honey. Spoon this mixture into each orange shell and decorate with the slivered almonds. Serve chilled.

STEWED FRUIT WITH CREAM: GUAVA/GOOSEBERRIES/ AMLA/FIG/APRICOT/BEETROOT

SERVES: 8   PREPARATION TIME: 1 HOUR

INGREDIENTS

Guava	8 pieces, slightly raw, medium and even-sized
Sugar	3½ cups
Water	2 cups
Cream	1 cup, lightly beaten
Bay leaf	2 leaves
Green cardamom powder	1 tsp

METHOD

Peel the guavas and cut into halves. Boil the water and then boil the guavas in it for 10 minutes. Let it cool. Then scoop out all the seeds with a spoon.

To make the sugar syrup for the stew, boil ½ cup water. Add the sugar, stirring continuously until all the sugar has been dissolved and the water has reduced to half the quantity. The sugar syrup is ready. Add the boiled guavas to this syrup and cook for 5 minutes with the bay leaves and the cardamom powder so that the sugar and the flavours of the spice seep into the guavas. The guava stew is ready to be served with lightly beaten cream.

Various other fruit can also be stewed and served with cream:

For **Gooseberry Stew**, use 500 grams of gooseberries. Wash and cook them with the sugar syrup.

For **Amla (Indian gooseberry) Stew**, use 16 pieces of amla. Add these to the boiling water and then drain all the water to remove the bitterness of the fruit. Follow the same recipe for the sugar syrup. **Fresh figs**, when in season can also be added to the Amla Stew a few minutes before the stew is cooked.

For **Beetroot Stew**, use 4 large ripe beetroots. Peel and cut them into small squares. Sauté the grated rind of 4 limes in a kadhai with 3 tablespoons of water until the water turns yellow. Add to it 1 cup of water and 1 cup of sugar. Let the sugar dissolve and the water reduce to half. Then add the beetroot chunks and cook for 5–7 minutes. Serve hot.

For **Apricot Stew**, you will need 500 grams of dried apricots with their stones. Mix the apricots with 100 grams of sugar and sufficient water to cover them. Soak overnight. The following day, parboil the apricots. Then follow the same recipe for the sugar syrup. Serve hot.

CHOCOLATE MAYONNAISE CAKE WITH CHOCOLATE FUDGE FROSTING

SERVES: 12   PREPARATION TIME: 1 HOUR

INGREDIENTS

Maida (Refined flour)	3 cups, unsifted
Baking powder	2¼ tsp
Baking soda	1½ tsp
Castor sugar	1½ cups
Cocoa	⅓ cup
Mayonnaise	1½ cups
Water	1½ cups
Vanilla essence	1½ tsp
Butter	1 tbsp

Note: The fresh mayonnaise used for this cake will be made without mustard powder and pepper (see page 219).

METHOD

Grease two (9×1½ inch) layer pans with 1 tablespoon of butter evenly on the base and the edges of the pan and line the bottom using butter paper (you may grease the butter paper with 1 tablespoon of butter and dust it with flour, forming a thin layer for easy removal).

In a large bowl, fold in the flour and the cocoa using a spatula. Then add the baking powder and the baking soda along with the castor sugar. Gradually pour water into this mixture, stirring continuously. Then add the freshly made mayonnaise (see page 219) and the vanilla essence and mix it until it is evenly smooth.

Pour this mixture into the prepared tins. Bake at 350°F/180°C for about 30 minutes. To check if the cake is done, insert a thin wooden skewer into the cake. It should come out clean, if not then let the cake bake until it is ready. Remove from the oven and keep aside for cooling.

INGREDIENTS FOR THE CHOCOLATE FUDGE FROSTING

To Make Unsweetened Chocolate:

Cocoa powder	9 tbsp, levelled
Butter	3 tbsp, melted

Mix these two ingredients to make the unsweetened chocolate.

To make sweetened chocolate fudge frosting:

Unsweetened chocolate	6 tbsp
Butter	½ cup
Milk	½ cup
Vanilla essence	1 tbsp
Castor sugar	1 cup or to taste

METHOD

In a pan, melt the butter and the unsweetened chocolate. Add the castor sugar along with the milk. Stir occasionally. Let it boil for 1 minute. As soon as it comes to a boil, mix in the vanilla essence and do not stir. After a minute transfer this to a glass or metal bowl.

Then separately, fill a large glass bowl with ice cubes and water. Place the bowl with the fudge frosting on top of the ice-filled bowl. Using a whisk, stir the fudge for 3–5 minutes, to achieve a smooth and thick consistency. The fudge frosting is ready to be used to ice the chocolate cake.

GUAVA CHEESE

SERVES: 8   PREPARATION TIME: 30 MINUTES

INGREDIENTS FOR GUAVA CHEESE

Guava	8 guavas, peeled, deseeded and cut into halves
Sugar	5 cups
Lime juice	5 tsp
Edible colour (red)	2 drops
Butter	1 tsp

METHOD

Grind the guava pieces into pulp. Measure out approximately 5 cups. Add an equal amount of sugar, approximately 5 cups, and 1 teaspoon of lime juice per cup of pulp, approximately 5 teaspoons.

Lightly grease a thick-bottomed saucepan. On a low flame, cook the pulp, sugar and the lime juice, stirring continuously until the sugar dissolves. Then add 2 drops of the edible red colour and 1 teaspoon of butter.

On a high flame, cook the mixture, stirring continuously, until it has the consistency of a soft ball. Pour into a greased platter, cool and then cut into squares. The guava cheese is ready to be served.

GUAVA JELLY

Guava	1 kg
Sugar	4 cups
Lime	4 tbsp
Water	4 cups (approx.)
Edible colour (red)	2 drops

METHOD

Wash the guavas. Remove the stem, peel and cut into halves. Put the guava pieces and water in a large vessel, cover and cook for half an hour, or until the pieces become tender. Let it cool.

Lift the pieces out of the vessel. Sieve the water and seeds through a muslin cloth and collect the water. Hang the muslin so that all the water gets drained. Measure the collected water. For every cup of water add a cup of sugar and a tablespoon of lime juice. Stirring continuously, cook on a low flame until all the sugar is dissolved.

Add 2 drops of edible red colour. On a high flame, cook for 15–20 minutes. Once the jelly has set, remove from the fire. Let it stand for 10 minutes. Then pour into a glass jar. Allow it to cool before covering. Serve it with cream or as a garnish on vanilla ice cream.

EVERYDAY ICE CREAM

SERVES: 6   PREPARATION TIME: 1 HOUR

INGREDIENTS

Milk	1 litre/4½ cups
Cornflour	1 tsp, heaped
Sugar	½ cup and 2 tbsp

METHOD

Boil the milk and allow it to thicken to almost half the original quantity. After one or two boils, add the sugar (approximately ½ a cup) and 1 teaspoon of cornflour and allow it to cook until it has thickened.

In a frying pan, caramelize 2 heaped tablespoons of sugar, until it turns a dark brown. Then add 2 tablespoons of milk and add this mixture to the thickened milk. Cool immediately by putting the pan in a bowl of cold water and freezing. When half frozen, take it out and beat it well. This will prevent any crystals from forming and the ice cream will have a smooth consistency. Freeze it again and serve.

This basic ice cream can be made into **Coffee Ice Cream** by adding 2 tablespoons of coffee after the milk has thickened.

To make **Mango Ice Cream**, add 2 large well-ripened mangoes, chopped into small squares. Add this to the half-frozen ice cream, mix it in well before refreezing it.

Drinks

Lucknow has a variety of traditional and seasonal sherbets (drinks) like Bel (Bengal quince) ka Sherbet and Falsay (Grewia Asiatica) ka Sherbet, known and consumed for their cooling effects and other health benefits. These are prepared in our homes during the scorching summer months, as is Kairi Aam ka Panna, the most delicious tangy drink made with raw mangoes, jaggery (gur) and Lahori Namak (rock salt).

Lassi is another staple drink consumed throughout India. It is made out of churned yoghurt which is either sweet or salty, depending on one's preference. Lucknow's Thandai is famous and its most famous vendor for almost a century has been Raja Thandai at Gol Darwaza in the Old City. It is a drink made out of milk and almonds and garnished with saffron. During Holi (the spring festival of colours), thandai is traditionally laced with bhang (hemp/cannabis) seeds, that can make the city around appear in kaleidoscopic colours!

Nimbu ka Sherbet (lime drink) in our home is made with our own garden-fresh limes and lemons that are used with their rinds and spiced with cumin powder, sugar and rock salt and garnished with fresh mint leaves. This simple drink is very refreshing and is a safeguard against sunstroke during the extreme heat of Indian summers.

KAIRI AAM KA PANNA
(RAW MANGO DRINK)

This is a refreshing summer beverage made of green mangoes (kairi). It is very cooling and prevents heatstroke.

SERVES: 10   PREPARATION TIME: 1 HOUR

INGREDIENTS

Kachha hara aam (raw green mangoes)	1kg
Powdered sugar	7 heaped tbsp
Jeera (cumin) powder	2 heaped tbsp
Sabut jeera (whole cumin) seeds	1 tsp, lightly roasted on a griddle
Pudina (mint)	30 leaves, fresh
Kaala namak (rock salt)	1 tsp

METHOD

Lightly roast the cumin seeds and grind them to get 2 heaped tablespoons of cumin powder.

Pressure cook the whole raw green mangoes in a little water. Then discard the water. You may also roast the green mangoes on an open fire or gas stove until lightly roasted on the outside. Peel the mangoes and squeeze to collect the pulp in a dish. Discard the seeds. Put the pulp in the freezer for about half an hour to chill.

Put together the chilled pulp, sugar, salt, cumin powder and the chopped mint leaves and mix well with a wooden spoon. Add a little water and then again mix well. The mixture should be pulpy. Pour over crushed ice and add chilled water to it. Serve garnished with whole mint leaves.

Note: You can prepare the pulp and freeze it for use as and when required.

BEL KA SHERBET
(SHERBET MADE OF BENGAL QUINCE)

SERVES: 8   PREPARATION TIME: 20 MINUTES

INGREDIENTS

Bel (Bengal quince)	1 fruit, peeled and pulp removed
Ice	10–12 cubes, crushed
Lime juice	1 tbsp
Water	4 glasses
Sugar	if required to further sweeten

METHOD

Mix the lime juice, sugar, water and ice in the bel paste. Grind together and the sherbet is ready. Serve chilled.

FALSAY KA SHERBET
(SHERBET MADE OF FALSA)

SERVES: 4   PREPARATION TIME: 10 MINUTES

INGREDIENTS

Falsay (Falsa)	1 kg, washed
Limes	4
Sugar	1 cup
Kaala namak (rock salt)	½ tsp
Water	3 cups

METHOD

Boil the falsa in the water. Strain through a fine sieve and extract all the juice by pressing the falsa pulp down with a spoon.

Put the pulp into a pan. Add the sugar and cook until it dissolves. Let it cool and add the juice of 4 limes and the rock salt. Pour into an ice tray and freeze.

For one medium glass of sherbet use 1 cube of the frozen falsa. Add chilled water, ice and stir. Serve chilled.

LASSI
(YOGHURT DRINK)

SERVES: 8   PREPARATION TIME: 15 MINUTES

INGREDIENTS

Dahi (yoghurt)	1 kg, fresh
Jeera (cumin seeds)	½ tbsp, roasted and powdered
Sugar	4 tbsp, for sweet lassi
Kaala namak (rock salt)	3 tsp, for namkeen/salted lassi

METHOD

In a blender, combine the yoghurt and the powdered cumin and blend until thoroughly mixed. Add sugar or salt. Serve chilled with crushed ice.

THANDAI
(MILK AND ALMOND SHERBET)

SERVES: 6   PREPARATION TIME: 30 MINUTES

INGREDIENTS

Milk	2½ cups, boiled
Badaam (almonds)	½ cup, soaked, drained and peeled
Khus-khus (poppy) seeds	2 tbsp
Magaz (musk melon) seeds	½ cup
Saunf (fennel) seeds	2 tbsp
Kaali mirch (black peppercorn)	1 tbsp
Hari elaichi (green cardamom)	10 pods
Sugar	1 cup
Rose petals	½ cup
Water	½ cup
Kesar (saffron)	6 strands

METHOD

Soak the fennel seeds, peppercorns and the green cardamom pods separately. Then grind them together with ½ a cup of water and strain through a muslin cloth. Separately grind the almonds into a smooth paste.

Soak the poppy seeds and musk melon seeds together. Strain and grind to a smooth paste. Grind the sugar and rose petals together.

Mix all the pastes together. Add milk and mix well. Sieve through a muslin cloth. Garnish with saffron. Serve chilled.

NIMBU KA SHERBET
(LEMON DRINK)

SERVES: 8   PREPARATION TIME: 10 MINUTES

INGREDIENTS

Nimbu (limes)	8 limes, unpeeled
Sugar	1 cup
Kaala namak (rock salt)	2 tsp
Water	1 litre
Salt	½ tsp
Pudina (mint) leaves	8 small sprigs, for garnishing

METHOD

Cut the limes into halves and remove the seeds. Put the lime halves, sugar, rock salt, salt and water in a blender for 3 minutes. Serve chilled. Garnish each glass with a sprig of mint.

Lucknowi Coffee, High Tea, Cocktail Snacks and Cakes

Like in many smaller towns, coffee parties were very popular in Lucknow. And because of the large British presence in Lucknow, high teas became regular features, as did cocktail parties. All these demi-meals in Lucknow had an assortment of savoury and sweet dishes. I think these are uniquely a Lucknow tradition, as they are also in many hill stations, such as in Mussoorie, where my parents established their second home.

My mother excelled in the making of a vast variety of these delicious snacks. The recipes in this cookbook are but a sampling of her endless inventions. She would often swap recipes with friends, but as was her habit she would add and subtract ingredients while making them. These recipes then became uniquely her own variations. In my mother's home, whether in Lucknow or Mussoorie, she was known for her Mutton Meatballs, Aloo ki Tikkis, Korma Sandwiches and her endless variety of cakes.

She has always been a superb baker and has taught baking to three generations of her family. In fact, the Basic Sponge Cake and the Chocolate Mayonnaise Cake in this cookbook were taught by her to her two great grandchildren, Anadya and Zohravar Singh Bhati. For this cookbook, Anadya helped her Badi Nanima by baking these herself for the photoshoot. Zohravar must have been seven years old when he learnt her version of a basic sponge cake. I remember as a young child, whenever he was required to bring a cake to school or take it to a picnic, he would quickly bake a cake himself. These are the genes inherited from my mother.

Apart from the Chocolate Mayonnaise Cake (see page 176 under Puddings) with its ultra-delicious fudge frosting, among my mother's trademark cakes are her Gooey Brownies. Through experimentation she realized that using peanut oil instead of butter made the brownies even gooier.

A favourite sandwich in my mother's home and mine are Korma Sandwiches. These are made with leftover mutton korma, with extra mustard powder and finely chopped spring onions added to it. Everybody relishes them. The important thing to remember for these sandwiches is that the korma itself has to be delicious.

Another leftover delicacy is Chicken or Mutton Chilli Fry. This recipe is from my school friend, Dr Indira Baptista Saxena. Indira told me that among Christians, after Christmas, this became a popular way of using leftover mutton and chicken roast. We do not wait for Christmas—we make it whenever we have leftover roast.

In our home, we often make different types of samosas for high teas and as cocktail snacks. Samosas are a Lucknow invention. Each one of our samosas has different ingredients and different spices, as given in the recipes. Our Aloo aur Bhuttey ki Golis covered in sesame seeds are also a house speciality.

MUTTON MEATBALLS

MAKES: 25 MEATBALLS   PREPARATION TIME: 30 MINUTES

INGREDIENTS

Mutton (minced)	½ kg, lean leg of mutton, well washed with all the water gently squeezed out
Eggs	2 lightly beaten
White onion	1 medium, finely chopped
Cheddar cheese	2 tbsp, grated
Garam masala (ground spices)	1 tbsp
Hara dhania (coriander)	20 leaves, finely chopped
Lime juice	1 tbsp
Oil	2 cups
Salt	1 tsp or to taste

METHOD

In a large bowl, mix the minced mutton with the white onions, fresh coriander leaves, eggs, cheese, garam masala, lime juice and salt. Keep aside for 15 minutes. Again mix thoroughly and with wet palms shape the mutton mixture into small balls.

On a high flame, heat the oil in a large frying pan and deep-fry the meatballs until they turn golden brown. Serve hot.

KEEMA SAMOSAS
(MINCED MEAT SAMOSAS)

MAKES: 25 SMALL SAMOSAS   PREPARATION TIME: 45 MINUTES

INGREDIENTS

Mutton mince (keema)	250 gms, minced from lean leg of mutton
Onion	1 large, finely chopped
Tomato	1 large, finely chopped
Hari mirch (green chilli)	1 deseeded and finely chopped
Hara dhania (coriander)	12 leaves, finely chopped

Adhrak (ginger) paste	1 tbsp
Lahsun (garlic) paste	1 tbsp
Haldi (turmeric) powder	1 tsp
Dhania (coriander) powder	1 tsp
Laal mirch (red chilli) powder	1 tsp
Garam masala (ground spices)	1 tbsp
Kalonji (onion) seeds	1 tsp
Sunflower oil	2 cups
Desi ghee	2 tbsp
Maida (refined flour)	250 gms
Salt	1 tsp or to taste

METHOD

Wash the minced mutton and let the water drain in a colander. Squeeze the excess water out with your palms.

Heat the oil in a kadhai and sauté the finely chopped onion and the ginger and garlic pastes along with the chopped tomato and green chilli. Then add the minced meat to this mixture with the powdered masalas and the salt. Cook the mince for 15 minutes, until the oil rises to the surface. Remove the excess oil from the mince with a spoon to make it dry for the filling. Then add the chopped coriander. The masala mince filling is ready. Set it aside and let it cool.

Knead the maida, desi ghee and kalonji together into a tight dough and divide into equal-sized portions. With a rolling pin, roll the dough into small rotis (5 inches each). Cut the roti into two semicircles. Then with your finger apply water along the cut edges, to moisten the surface and fold the semicircles into the shape of a cone, folding from both sides. Overlap and press the sides to seal them. Form the cones one by one and fill them with the mince masala, ensuring that there is no overfilling. Again wet your finger and seal the edges after filling them.

On a medium-high flame, heat the oil in a kadhai and fry the samosas until they turn golden brown. Serve hot with fresh Mint Chutney (see page 206).

MATAR SAMOSAS
(PEA SAMOSAS)

MAKES: 30 SMALL SAMOSAS   PREPARATION TIME: 30 MINUTES

INGREDIENTS

Matar (peas)	250 gms, fresh tender peas
Onion	1 large, finely chopped
Hari mirch (green chilli)	1 finely chopped
Adhrak (ginger) paste	1 tsp
Lahsun (garlic) paste	1 tsp
Haldi (turmeric) powder	1 tsp
Garam masala (ground masala)	1 tsp
Amchoor (dry mango) powder	1 tsp
Kalonji (onion) seeds	1 tsp
Hara dhania (coriander)	12 leaves, finely chopped
Maida (refined flour)	250 gms
Sunflower oil	2 cups, for frying
Desi ghee	2 tbsp
Salt	1 tsp or to taste

METHOD

Wash the tender peas and strain in a colander. In a large saucepan, heat the oil and add the finely chopped onion and green chilli and sauté until it turns golden brown. Add the ginger and garlic pastes and the peas. Then add all the powdered masalas with the salt and cook in ½ cup of water, until the water is completely absorbed. Add the finely chopped coriander leaves. The masala peas filling is ready. Keep it aside to let it cool.

Knead the maida, desi ghee and kalonji together into a tight dough and divide into equal-sized portions. With a rolling pin, roll the dough into small rotis (5 inches each), then cut each roti into two semicircles. Then with your finger apply water along the cut edges, to moisten the surface and fold the semicircles into the shape of a cone, folding from both sides. Overlap and press the sides to seal them. Form the cones one by one and fill them with the masala peas, ensuring that there is no overfilling. Again wet your finger and seal the edges after filling the cones.

On a medium-high flame, heat the oil in a kadhai and fry the samosas until they turn golden brown. Matar samosas are ready to be served with mint and coriander chutney.

ALOO SAMOSAS
(POTATO SAMOSAS)

MAKES: 24 SMALL SAMOSAS   PREPARATION TIME: 30 MINUTES

INGREDIENTS

Aloo (potatoes)	4 medium, peeled, roasted and cut into small squares
Onion	1 large, finely chopped
Hari mirch (green chilli)	1 chilli, finely chopped
Adhrak (ginger)	1 piece, finely chopped
Lahsun (garlic)	4 cloves, finely chopped
Jeera (cumin) seeds	1 tsp, roasted
Saunf (fennel) seeds	1 tsp
Haldi (turmeric) powder	1 tsp
Garam masala (ground masala)	1 tbsp
Amchoor (dry mango) powder	1 tsp
Kalonji (onion) seeds	1 tsp
Hara dhania (coriander)	12 leaves, finely chopped
Maida (refined flour)	250 gms
Sunflower oil	2 cups, for frying
Desi ghee	2 tbsp
Salt	1 tsp or to taste

METHOD

In a large saucepan, heat the oil and add the cumin seeds until they turn slightly brown and release an aroma. Add the finely chopped onion, green chillies and the chopped ginger and garlic. Then add all the powdered masalas with the salt. Sauté the mixture until it turns lightly brown. Add the roasted potato squares with the fennel seeds. Cook for 5 minutes. Then, add the finely chopped coriander leaves to the mixture. The masala potatoes filling is ready. Keep it aside to let it cool.

Knead the maida, desi ghee and kalonji together into a tight dough and divide into equal-sized portions. With a rolling pin, roll the dough into small rotis (5 inches each), then cut each roti into two semicircles. Then with your finger apply water along the cut edges, to moisten the surface and fold the semicircles into the shape of a cone, folding from both sides. Overlap and press the sides to seal them. Form the cones one by one and fill them with the masala potatoes, ensuring that there is no overfilling. Again wet your finger and seal the edges after filling them.

On a medium-high flame, heat the oil in a kadhai and fry the samosas until they turn golden brown. Serve hot with mint and coriander chutney.

ALOO AUR BHUTTEY KI GOLI
(POTATO AND CORN BALLS)

SERVES: 8   PREPARATION TIME: 30 MINUTES

INGREDIENTS

Aloo (potatoes)	3 large, boiled and mashed
Bhutta dana (sweetcorn kernels)	½ cup
White onion	1 small, finely chopped
Hari mirch (green chilli)	1 deseeded, finely chopped
Hara dhania (coriander)	12 leaves, finely chopped
Kaali mirch (black peppercorns)	10 freshly ground and powdered
Garam masala (ground spices)	1 tbsp
Egg	1 egg white
Maida (refined flour)	4 tbsp
Safed til (white sesame) seeds	50 gms
Lime juice	1 tbsp
Sunflower oil	2 cups

Salt   1 tsp or to taste

METHOD

Mash the potatoes and mix with the sweetcorn, chopped onion, green chilli, coriander leaves, peppercorns, garam masala, egg white, lime juice and salt and shape the mixture into small- to medium-sized round balls.

On a flat dish, mix and spread the maida and the white sesame seeds. Then roll the balls on this mixture, so that it evenly coats the balls. In a kadhai, heat the oil and fry the balls, until they turn golden brown. Serve hot with mint and coriander chutney.

ALOO KI TIKKI
(POTATO PATTIES)

SERVES: MAKES 12 TIKKIS   PREPARATION TIME: 40 MINUTES

INGREDIENTS

Aloo (potatoes)	4 large, boiled and mashed
Hari mirch (green chilli)	2–3 deseeded and minced
Pudina/Dhania (mint/coriander) leaves	2 tbsp, finely chopped
Bread	4 slices
Dhania (coriander) powder	½ tsp
Laal mirch (red chilli) powder	½ tsp
Kaali mirch (black pepper) powder	½ tsp
Amchoor (dry mango) powder	½ tsp
Jeera (cumin) powder	½ tsp
Sunflower oil	2 cups, for frying
Salt	1 tsp or to taste

METHOD

Soak the bread in water, then squeeze and mix the bread pulp with the potatoes and the rest of the ingredients, except the oil. Take a small portion of the mixture, flatten it out on your palm and form small round patties.

In a kadhai, heat the oil and then deep-fry the patties until golden brown. Remove from the kadhai with a perforated frying spoon. Then place them on paper towels to remove the excess oil. Serve hot with fresh Mint Chutney (see page 206 under Chutneys).

KORMA SANDWICHES

MAKES: 24 SMALL SQUARE SANDWICHES   PREPARATION TIME: 15 MINUTES

INGREDIENTS

Mutton	1 cup, deboned, mutton pieces removed from the korma (curry)
Korma Curry	½ cup
Bread	multigrain, 1 loaf of 8–12 slices
Onion	1 small, finely chopped
Hara dhania (coriander)	12 leaves, finely chopped
Hari mirch (green chilli)	1 deseeded and finely chopped
Mustard powder	1 tsp
Lettuce	2 leaves, washed and dried, for garnishing

METHOD

Mix all the ingredients except the lettuce into the finely chopped mutton. Then add 3 tablespoons of mutton curry. Mix well and spread evenly on the slices to make the sandwiches. Cut off the sides and divide each sandwich into four small, equal-sized squares.

Refrigerate the sandwiches, covered with a wet well-wrung out muslin cloth, to keep them fresh. Just before serving, finely chop the lettuce lengthwise and garnish the sandwiches with it. The Korma Sandwiches are ready to be served.

CHICKEN/MUTTON CHILLI FRY

SERVES: 8   PREPARATION TIME: 30 MINUTES

INGREDIENTS

Chicken/Mutton	2 cups, shredded from the roast (see page 102)
Onions	2 large, thinly sliced
Tomatoes	2 medium, cut into cubes
Garlic	1 tsp, finely chopped
Ginger	1 tsp, finely chopped
Green chilli	4 deseeded and finely chopped
Vinegar	1 tbsp
Egg	1
Oil	2 tbsp

METHOD

Heat the oil in a saucepan and sauté the onions. Add the ginger, garlic and the green chillies and lightly fry the mixture. Add the chicken or mutton and stir in for 1 minute with the cubed tomatoes. Then add the egg, stirring continuously.

When well fried, remove from the flame and add the vinegar. Leave on a low flame for 30 seconds. Serve hot.

GOOEY BROWNIES

SERVES: 10   PREPARATION TIME: 40 MINUTES

INGREDIENTS

Cocoa	6 tbsp
Flour	¾ cup, sifted
Baking powder	½ tsp
Eggs	2 at room temperature
Sugar	1 cup
Vanilla essence	1 tsp

Butter	½ cup
Walnuts	1 cup, coarsely chopped
Salt	½ tsp

METHOD

Dissolve the cocoa in a little hot water, then melt the butter and mix it with the cocoa. Let it cool.

Sift the flour with the baking powder and salt. Beat the eggs until light. Add the sugar, then the cocoa mixture and fold it in. Add the flour, vanilla essence and the walnuts. Bake in a greased pan (8×8 inches) in a moderately hot oven 350°F/180°C for 30–40 minutes. Let it cool before cutting into squares and serving.

Note: For extra soft and chewy brownies, make them with ½ cup of peanut oil instead of the butter. These brownies can be served with home-made vanilla ice cream (see page 179).

DATE AND WALNUT CAKE

SERVES: 10   PREPARATION TIME: 40 MINUTES

INGREDIENTS

Khajur (Dates)	2 cups, coarsely chopped
Akhrot (walnuts)	½ cup, coarsely chopped
Flour	½ cup, sifted
Eggs	4, at room temperature
Sugar	½ cup
Vanilla essence	½ tsp
Baking powder	½ tsp

METHOD

Beat the eggs until they become foamy. Add the sugar and vanilla essence and stir them in until they are well mixed. Then fold in the flour and the baking powder. Gradually add the dates and walnuts, stirring gently.

Bake the mixture in a greased pan (8x8 inches) in a moderately hot oven 350°F/180°C for 30–40 minutes. Let it cool before cutting into squares and serving.

Note: This cake can be served with whipped cream.

EGGLESS SPICY CAKE

SERVES: 10   PREPARATION TIME: 1 HOUR

INGREDIENTS

Butter	4 tbsp
Stewed apple	1 cup
Nutmeg	½ tsp, ground
Cinnamon powder	½ tsp
Cocoa	1 tsp
Flour	1½ cups, sifted
Sugar	4 tbsp
Soda bicarbonate	1 tsp
Baking powder	1 tsp
Lime juice	1 tsp

METHOD

Cream the butter and sugar. Add the warm apple with soda bicarbonate mixed in it. Then stir in the sifted flour and baking powder, cocoa and the spices. Mix in the fruit.

Pour the mixture in a lined and greased 7-inch cake tin. Bake for 1 hour in an oven heated to 300°F/150°C. Remove from the tin. When cooled, dust the surface with ground cinnamon and a few drops of lime juice.

APPLE SPONGE CAKE

SERVES: 8–10   PREPARATION TIME: 40 MINUTES

INGREDIENTS

Cooking apples	2 large, peeled, cored and grated
Refined flour	1 cup
Butter	¼ cup
Egg	1 at room temperature
Castor sugar	¼ cup
Baking powder	1 tsp
Milk	1 tbsp
Lime peel	2 rinds
Orange juice/ Marmalade	1 tbsp
Salt	1 tsp

METHOD

Sift together the flour, baking powder and the salt. Then beat the butter and sugar together. Add the egg and beat well. Add the flour mixture, a little at a time, and mix well. While adding the flour, add a little milk from time to time so that the mixture is of a dropping consistency. Pour into a greased pie dish.

Sprinkle the grated apples over the sponge mixture with the lime peel and orange juice or with the marmalade. Drench liberally with castor sugar. Bake in a moderately hot oven (350°F/180°C) for 30 minutes. Serve with cream.

CARROT CAKE

SERVES: 8   PREPARATION TIME: 1 HOUR

INGREDIENTS

Carrots	1 cup, grated
Wheat flour	1 cup

Sugar	1 cup, brown or castor
Refined oil	¾ cup
Eggs	2 at room temperature
Raisins	½ cup (optional)

METHOD

Mix all the ingredients together in a mixer. Pour this mixture into an 8-inch greased cake pan. Bake in the oven for 30–40 minutes at 350°F/180° C. Serve hot.

BASIC SPONGE CAKE

SERVES: 8   PREPARATION TIME: 30 MINUTES

INGREDIENTS

Maida (Refined flour)	3 cups
Eggs	3 at room temperature
Sugar	½ cup
Baking powder	2 tbsp
Refined oil	1 tbsp
Hot water	2 tbsp

METHOD

Beat the eggs and sugar until peaks are formed. Add the flour and baking powder. Stir gradually and then add the oil and hot water.

Pour the mixture into an 8-inch greased pan. Bake in a hot oven of 480°F/250°C for 10–15 minutes. The sponge cake is ready and can be served hot.

BUTTER COOKIES

SERVES: 10–12   PREPARATION TIME: 30 MINUTES

INGREDIENTS

Flour	500 gms
Baking powder	1½ tsp
Sugar	150 gms
Vanilla sugar	2 tsp
Salt	a pinch
Eggs	2
Egg white	1
Egg yolk	1
Unsalted butter	250 gms, cold
Icing sugar	2 tbsp, to sprinkle (for the egg glaze)

For Chocolate Glaze:

Dark cooking chocolate	250 gms
Icing sugar	60 gms
Warm Water	4 tbsp

METHOD

Sift the flour and baking powder together onto a clean work surface. Make a little well in the centre and pour the sugar, vanilla sugar, salt, eggs and egg white into it. Work the mixture into a thick paste with a part of the flour in the centre. Put in the cold, chopped butter and knead together to make a large dough ball. Now, from the centre, combine all the ingredients together and knead. If the dough becomes too sticky to manage, refrigerate briefly and then resume the kneading. You should obtain a smooth dough.

To make plain butter cookies, roll the dough out thinly and cut out round cookies with cookie-cutters. Beat 1 egg yolk and brush the cookies with the liquid. Place the cookies on a greased baking tray and bake in an oven at 350°F/180°C for about 15 minutes until they turn golden. Before serving, sprinkle the cookies with the icing sugar through a fine sieve.

To make chocolate cookies, follow the same procedure as above, omitting the egg yolk glaze.

Mix the dark cooking chocolate, water and icing sugar and mix well to make the chocolate glaze. After baking, dip the cookies in this warm chocolate glaze. Let cool completely and then serve.

PLAIN SCONES

MAKES: 12–15 SCONES   PREPARATION TIME: 45 MINUTES

INGREDIENTS

Maida (all-purpose flour)	500 gms, plus extra for dusting
Wheatgerm flour	½ cup (optional)
Baking powder	2 heaped tbsp
Castor sugar	2 heaped tbsp
Unsalted butter	100 gms, cut into pieces, plus extra for greasing the pan
Whole milk	1½ cups
Egg	1 beaten
Salt	1 tbsp
Whipped double cream/Butter and jam	

METHOD

Pre-heat the oven to 400°F/200°C and grease a baking tray with butter, or use baking parchment.

Sift the plain flour into a bowl and add the wheatgerm flour, if using. Mix in the baking powder, sugar and salt, then add the butter and rub it in with your fingers until the mixture resembles fresh breadcrumbs.

Make a well in the middle, pour in exactly 300 millilitres (1½ cups) of milk and use a fork to work it into the dry ingredients. Finish by hand but without overworking the mixture. Lightly bring everything together to form a soft but firm dough. If it is too dry add a little more milk. If it is too wet add some more flour. It must not be sticky at all.

On a lightly floured surface, pat or roll the dough into a solid shape about 3 centimetres (1¼ inches) thick. Using a 2-inch cutter, cut the dough into rounds and place them individually on the greased baking tray. Glaze the tops with the beaten egg and bake for 15–20 minutes until they turn a light golden brown. Serve warm with whipped double cream or butter and jam.

PINEAPPLE AND MANGO COMPOTE

SERVES: 6–8   PREPARATION TIME: 15 MINUTES

INGREDIENTS

Fresh pineapple	500 gms, diced
Mango	2 large, diced
Lime juice	1 tbsp
Rum	1 tbsp
Castor sugar	2 tbsp
Ginger	1-inch piece, juiced

METHOD

Lightly blend all the ingredients into a coarse purée. Refrigerate.

Chill well before serving in individual short tumblers or large ramekins. Garnish with a mixture of finely diced pineapple and mango. Decorate with a sprig of mint.

Chutneys, Pickles, Murabbas

All of India excels in chutneys, pickles and murabbas. Each region has its own distinct and delicious specialities. The particular recipes in this section are from Lucknow. Pudina (mint) Chutney is served every day in our homes. The Kairi ki Meethi Chutney is seasonal, as the raw mangoes are available only during the early summer months. So is the Aam ka Khatta Meetha Achaar, although, if well preserved, it can last for months. Our home-made Tomato Chutney can be made with or without dates and is a great accompaniment to any meal.

My mother's Hari Mirchi (green chilli) Achaar, seasoned with numerous ingredients, has been a delight for all those who have a spicy palate, such as myself. Our Nimbu ka Achaar is made with our own home-grown fragrant limes. The freshest organic ingredients always produce the best results.

PUDINA CHUTNEY
(FRESH MINT CHUTNEY)

SERVES: 8   PREPARATION TIME: 10 MINUTES

INGREDIENTS

Pudina (fresh mint) leaves	250 gms, leaves without the stems
Hari mirch (green chilli)	5–6 pieces, to taste
Imli (tamarind) paste/	2 tbsp
Amchoor (dry mango) powder	2 tbsp
Salt	to taste
Lime juice	2 limes

METHOD

Grind all the ingredients together on a grindstone. Alternatively, use an electric mixer. The Pudina Chutney is ready to be served.

KAIRI KI MEETHI CHUTNEY
(SWEET RAW MANGO CHUTNEY)

SERVES: 8   PREPARATION TIME: 15 MINUTES

INGREDIENTS

Kairi (raw green mangoes)	1 kg, peeled and finely chopped or grated
Gur or sugar	1½ cup
Ginger	1½ tbsp, finely sliced
Red chillies	10 whole
Kalonji	1 tsp
Raisins	15 soaked in hot water
White vinegar	½ cup
Limes	2 juiced
Salt	to taste

METHOD

Combine all the ingredients except the limes in a stainless steel pan.

The Lucknow Cookbook

Cook on low heat, stirring occasionally with a wooden spoon until the liquid thickens. Remove from the flame and let it cool.

When completely cooled, add the lime juice as it preserves the chutney. Store in a glass jar. Do not use a wet or soiled spoon in the chutney.

AAMLA KA MURABBA
(INDIAN GOOSEBERRY PRESERVE)

MAKES: 40 PIECES   PREPARATION TIME: 35 MINUTES

INGREDIENTS

Aamla (Indian gooseberry)	1 kg, large
Sugar	1½ kg
Salt	2 tbsp
Lime	1 washed and cut into quarters

METHOD

Wash the aamlas and soak them in salted water for 2 days. This makes the skin firm for preserving or else it will break when the aamlas are boiled.

Drain the aamlas and prick them all over with a fork. Add enough water to cover the aamlas and boil them for 3–4 minutes. Drain.

For the syrup:

Boil approximately 2 cups of water in a pan, add the sugar and limes and bring to a boil. Remove the scum.

Bring the syrup to a boil again and continue to cook until it is of a two-string consistency. Add the boiled aamla and cook for 2–3 minutes. Remove from the flame and let it cool. Transfer the contents to a sterilized airtight glass jar. Secure a square of muslin around the mouth of the jar and leave it to mature for 2 days. Then replace the muslin with the lid of the jar.

Note: If serving as a dessert, add blanched and peeled almond halves and serve along with lightly whipped cream.

TOMATO CHUTNEY WITH DATES

SERVES: 8–10   PREPARATION TIME: 20 MINUTES

INGREDIENTS

Tomatoes	1 kg
Khajur (dates)	250 gms
Karhi patta (curry leaf)	10–12 small leaves
Gur (jaggery)	100 gms
Hari mirch (green chilli)	5 pieces
Onions	2 finely chopped
Lahsun (garlic) paste	1½ tsp
Adhrak (ginger) paste	1½ tsp
Haldi (turmeric) powder	1½ tsp
Dhania (coriander) powder	1½ tsp
Laal mirch (red chillies)	4 whole
Oil	2 tbsp

METHOD

Heat the oil, add the curry leaves and let them sputter. Then put in the onions, ginger and garlic pastes, all the masalas and the chillies along with the (jaggery) and ½ a cup of water, making sure that the jaggery melts evenly with the masalas.

Add the finely chopped tomatoes and cook on a low flame for 20 minutes. Then add the dates (with the seeds), cut into halves. Cook for 10 minutes. The Tomato Chutney is ready to be served. The chutney can be stored in a glass jar and refrigerated, as it can last up to a month.

AAM KA KHATTA MEETHA ACHAAR
(SWEET AND SOUR MANGO PICKLE)

MAKES: 750 ML

PREPARATION TIME: 30 MINUTES

COOKING TIME: 1 HOUR 45 MINUTES

INGREDIENTS

Kachcha aam (raw green mangoes)	1 kg
Lahsun (garlic)	1 whole bulb, separated and peeled
Adhrak (ginger)	10 pieces, finely sliced
Gur (jaggery)	250 gms
Sookhi laal mirch (dry red chilli)	50 gms, whole chillies slit at one end
Laal mirch (red chilli) powder	1 tsp
Jeera (cumin)	1 tsp
Saunf (fennel)	1 tbsp
Kalonji (onion) seeds	1 tsp
Dhania (coriander) powder	1 tsp
Methi (fenugreek) seeds	1 tsp
Sabut dhania (coriander) seeds	1 tbsp
Haldi (turmeric) powder	1 tsp
Sarson (mustard) oil	1 cup
Salt	1 tsp

Optional: To enhance the look of the pickle, if available, use a whole bulb of Pahari Lahsun also called Kashmiri Lahsun or Snow Mountain garlic. This variety has fat cloves of garlic.

METHOD

Heat the oil and let it cool. Then put the pieces of the raw mangoes in the oil and add to it all the masalas together with the salt. Then add 2 cups of water and boil 15 minutes.

At the end of this process add the jaggery and cook for 5 minutes only, until the jaggery melts. Let the mixture cool completely. Transfer the pickle to a glass jar.

NIMBU KA ACHAAR
(LIME PICKLE)

MAKES: 500 ML   PREPARATION: 1 HOUR

INGREDIENTS

Whole limes	24
Lime juice	24 limes, juiced
Adhrak (ginger)	50 gms, finely julienned
Lahsun (garlic)	5 cloves, thinly sliced
Sarson (mustard seeds)	1 tbsp
Laal mirch (red chilli) powder	50 gms
Jeera (cumin) seeds	1 tbsp
Haldi (turmeric) powder	1 tsp
Hari mirch (green chilli)	5 whole
Vinegar	1 cup
Lahori namak (rock salt)/Salt	250 gms

METHOD

Boil the lemons until they change colour and their bitter oil rises to the surface. Remove this oil.

Remove from the flame and drain. Spread the limes out on a clean cloth in the open for a day. The next day, cut each lime into four pieces.

Roast the spices separately and mix them with salt. Also mix in the julienned ginger and garlic. Add to the limes and put the mixture along with the green chillies in a big glass jar. Mix the vinegar with the lime juice and pour over the mixture already in the jar. Keep the jar in the sun for a day or two. The pickle is ready.

HARI MIRCH KA ACHAAR
(GREEN CHILLI PICKLE)

MAKES: 1 KG   PREPARATION TIME: 1 HOUR

INGREDIENTS

Hari mirch (green chilli)	1½ kg, small and even-sized
Limes	750 gms, juiced
Laal mirch (red chilli) powder	2 tsp
Methi (fenugreek) seeds	3½ cups, ground
Saunf (fennel) seeds	2 tbsp
Dark rye (mustard) seeds	3½ cups, coarsely ground
Kalonji (onion) seeds	2 tbsp
Vinegar	1 cup
Sugar	3 tbsp
Salt	1 cup

METHOD

Slit the green chillies lengthwise, remove the seeds and then stuff them
with the ground masalas and salt. Transfer them into a glass jar. Add
the fennel and onion seeds. Pour the lime juice, sugar and vinegar on
top of the chillies. Shake the jar to mix the ingredients together. Let it
mature for two days and then it is ready to be served.

Note: The jar should be large enough so that the ingredients can be shaken
together.

ALOO AUR HARI MIRCH KA ACHAAR
(POTATO AND GREEN CHILLI PICKLE)

MAKES: 1 KG

PREPARATION TIME: 20 MINUTES

COOKING TIME: 25 MINUTES

INGREDIENTS

Potatoes	500 gms, large, cut into small squares
Hari mirch (green chilli)	150 gms
Laal mirch (red chilli) powder	2 tsp
Haldi (turmeric) powder	1 tsp
Dhania (coriander) powder	1 tsp
Jeera (cumin) powder	1 tsp
Sugar	½ cup
Vinegar	2 tbsp
Sunflower oil	1 cup
Salt	1 tbsp

FOR TEMPERING:

Jeera (cumin) seeds	1 tsp
Kaali sarson (black mustard) seeds	1 tsp
Kalonji (onion) seeds	½ tsp
Methi (fenugreek) seeds	½ tsp
Adhrak (ginger) paste	1 tsp
Lahsun (garlic) paste	1 tsp

METHOD

Boil the potatoes, then peel and cut them into 1-inch square pieces. Wash the chillies. Leaving a little stem on the chillies, slit along one side.

Heat the oil and fry the potatoes until they are golden. Keep them aside in a bowl.

Fry the green chillies until they wilt just a little and there is a slight change in colour. Remove these and add them to the fried potatoes. Add the sugar, vinegar, salt, chilli powder, turmeric, cumin and coriander powders to the potatoes and the chillies.

Reheat the oil in which the potatoes and green chillies were fried. Add cumin and mustard seeds. When the mustard begins to pop, add the onion and fenugreek seeds. A few seconds later, add the ginger and garlic paste. Fry for a minute or two. Remove from the fire and allow it to cool. When cooled, add it to the potatoes and the green chillies.

Transfer the pickle to a dry, clean airtight jar. This unusual pickle is ready but it only keeps well for a week or two.

CUCUMBER RELISH

MAKES: 1 KG   PREPARATION TIME: 3 HOURS

INGREDIENTS

Cucumber	20 large, unpeeled and thinly sliced into rounds
Onions	4 medium, cut into rounds
Mustard seeds	1½ tbsp
Kaali mirch (peppercorn)	1 tbsp, whole
Tejpatta (bay leaf)	2–3 small leaves
Laung (cloves)	8–10
Vinegar	5 cups
Sugar	5 cups
Salt	¾ cup

METHOD

In a large basin, arrange three alternating layers of cucumber rounds and onions. Sprinkle salt over each layers and cover with ice cubes. Cover the basin with a fine muslin cloth for 3 hours.

In a pan add the sugar, vinegar, mustard seeds, whole pepper and bay leaf. Mix the ingredients together and boil. Remove from the flame before the mixture starts to bubble.

Then drain the cucumber and onion mixture and add into the boiled mixture. Boil once more, but remove from the fire before the mixture reaches bubbling point. Remove it from the fire and let it cool. Transfer to a glass jar and refrigerate.

Note: This relish is delicious with Lucknow's Anglo-Indian food. When chopped and added to egg sandwiches, it adds a piquant flavour.

Home-made and Organic

These recipes are everyday essentials. Of these, Dahi ki Paneer, which is hung yoghurt cheese, is extensively used in our homes. My mother prepares many different types of mayonnaise, used for different purposes. The recipe for mayonnaise in this cookbook is a basic recipe, which I consider better than any commercial one. This recipe has been used by Anadya, my mother's great-granddaughter, to make the most delicious Chocolate Mayonnaise Cake for the photo shoot for this book.

PANEER
(INDIAN COTTAGE CHEESE)

MAKES: APPROXIMATELY 500 GMS   PREPARATION TIME: 15 MINUTES +
                                                          3 HOURS TO SET

INGREDIENTS

Milk	3 litres
Lime juice	6 tbsp

METHOD

In a large saucepan, boil the milk, stirring occasionally. Do not allow any cream to form on the top. When the milk is about to boil, stir in the lime juice. The milk will begin to curdle immediately and the whey will separate. When that happens, strain the curdled milk through a muslin cloth.

Hang the muslin cloth for approximately an hour, to allow all the water to drain out completely from the fresh paneer. To make a block of paneer, wrap it in a muslin cloth and place a heavy weight on top to compress it. Keep aside for 3 hours. The block may be cut into cubes or rectangular pieces, to be fried and eaten or used in vegetables. Refrigerate the paneer in a bowl filled with water that covers it, to keep it soft and fresh.

Note: Keep the whey to add to vegetables or dals in lieu of water.

DAHI KI PANEER
(COTTAGE CHEESE MADE WITH HUNG YOGHURT)

MAKES: APPROXIMATELY 250 GMS   PREPARATION TIME: 3 HOURS

INGREDIENTS

Yoghurt	1 kg, two days old

METHOD

Put the yoghurt in a clean muslin cloth and hang it with a pan below. It will take 2–3 hours for all the water to drain out. When the water has drained completely, scrape the cheese off the cloth and place it in a bowl. Refrigerate and use as and when required.

Note: This fresh cheese is excellent as a paratha filling with finely chopped green onions and green chillies mixed with salt, pepper and roasted cumin.

It can also be cooked as a side dish with salt, a pinch of red chilli powder and 2 tablespoons of finely chopped onions, green chillies and fresh coriander leaves. These should all be added to the hung paneer in a frying pan with 1 teaspoon of oil and cooked for 5 minutes on a medium flame.

Hung dahi ki paneer also makes an excellent dip. Whip it with a fork, season it with salt and freshly ground peppercorns, ½ a teaspoon of fresh garlic juice and 1 tablespoon each of finely cut green chillies, spring onions and fresh coriander leaves.

WHITE BUTTER

MAKES: 500 GMS   PREPARATION TIME: 1 HOUR

INGREDIENTS

Dahi (yoghurt)	2 kg
Salt	2 tbsp

METHOD

Churn the yoghurt with a wooden churner in a large deep vessel. When the yoghurt starts frothing, remove the froth and collect it in a muslin cloth. Repeat this process several times until the butter separates from the yoghurt and stops frothing. The leftover residual water is buttermilk. Collect the butter from the muslin cloth. To make the butter salty, add salt while churning the yoghurt.

Note: The leftover buttermilk is very nutritious and makes a popular summer drink tempered with salt, pepper, roasted cumin and fresh curry leaves. Buttermilk can also be used for cooking vegetables.

DESI GHEE
(CLARIFIED BUTTER)

MAKES: 300 GMS   TIME 2 HOURS

INGREDIENTS

Unsalted white butter   500 gms

METHOD

In a heavy-bottomed pan over a low flame, heat and fully melt the unsalted butter without letting it brown. Then increase the flame and bring the butter to a boil. When the butter starts foaming, stir once and reduce to a low flame.

Simmer gently for about 45 minutes until the milk solids settle on the bottom of the pan and the transparent butter is floating on the surface. Drain the transparent butter, i.e. desi ghee, through the muslin cloth into another container without disturbing the sediment. Once cool, it will solidify. Store at room temperature.

KHOYA
(WHOLE MILK FUDGE)

MAKES: 300 GMS   PREPARATION TIME: 1½ HRS

INGREDIENTS

Milk   2 litres (fresh and full fat)

METHOD

In a kadhai or in a non-stick saucepan, pour in the milk and allow it to come to a boil. Then reduce the flame. Stir the milk constantly, until it thickens and reduced to half the quantity. Continue stirring the milk and keep scraping off and removing the dried layer of milk that forms on the sides of the kadhai. This is a precaution against the milk getting a burnt flavour.

Keep stirring until the milk becomes dense like halwa. Refrigerate the khoya for 3–4 days or it can be frozen to last up to a month. Use in Meetha and Lucknowi cuisine as required.

MAYONNAISE

MAKES: 1½ CUPS   PREPARATION TIME: 20 MINUTES

INGREDIENTS

Eggs	2 yolks at room temperature
Mustard powder	1 tsp
Castor sugar	1 tsp
Salt	$^1/_2$ tsp
Kaali mirch (black pepper) powder	1 tsp
Lime juice	1 tbsp
Salad oil/Olive oil	1 cup
Vinegar	1 tbsp

METHOD

Using an electric beater, blend the egg yolks with the mustard powder, castor sugar, salt and black pepper. Slowly add the oil drop by drop, beating continuously until half the oil is used. The remaining half of the oil may be added faster, until the mayonnaise thickens. Add the lime juice and then gradually add the vinegar while beating.

The mayonnaise should be of a thick consistency like double cream. If it is too thick, it can be slightly thinned down by adding 2 tablespoons of beaten yoghurt.

Memory and Remembrance

RAVI TREHAN

Childhood is measured out by sounds and smells and sights,
before the dark hour of reason grows.
—John Betjeman

Memories of Lucknow are a constant source of solace to me as I live and age in another land. The sky dense with birds and kites competing for dominance are ever present in my mind's eye. But, decades on, the delights of the palate are what overwhelm my memories. And it's my Aunty Chan [Chand Sur] who gets the prize for that!

As I look back on my childhood, I realize I had created a competition in my mind about where I would indulge myself each day. The tradition of four culinary events of breakfast, lunch, tea and dinner were rigorously followed. Breakfast was always at home, since skipping out so early was too much of a betrayal to the activity at the house. My options for dinner were limited as well. I did not have the authority of an adult to manoeuvre the venue. My freedom to choose was confined to the lunch or tea slots. By late morning the urge to visit my aunt's house would set in.

On reaching my aunt's place, I would be warmly greeted by Ashok's dog. Depending on who was in the house, I would float from room to room, be given advice by my uncle, rummage through the books, promise to return them once read, and largely settle in and let time pass.

Around lunchtime, the play was always the same. My aunt would insist I telephone her sister informing her of my decision to stay for lunch. My mother never sounded terribly pleased, as I guess she felt I was indicating a preference. The dishes were delectable and I would eat with all the gusto I could muster. One staple was a garlic yoghurt serving and I still ask for that. The elders would invariably take their afternoon nap, my cousins might lie down for a while, but I would continue to potter around and somehow always manage to reappear at teatime.

Teatime had an exotic element to it. Lunch was usually an Indian meal. Dinner could be a light Indian-English composition finished off with a chocolate soufflé. I had understood that rhythm and there was a familiarity about it that didn't make the heart beat any faster.

My aunt's tea did that to me. I knew it would be deliciously sweet but what would it be? Only today do I understand the range of her baking expertise. My penchant for high tea remains as I continue to chase scones at the Ritz, meringues at the Dorchester, or cookies at the Four Seasons in New York. But I almost always remember my aunt's unparalleled touch.

I sometimes wonder what I would do without these memories. My life in my aunt's house and my mother's home centred on the warmth of food and family. Lucknow was for me a celebration of food. And my aunt defined those heights of culinary Lucknow.

Acknowledgments

There are many people to thank, both family and our friends. First, my brother, Ashok, for gathering family photographs, particularly ones of our mother. And for finding another treasure trove—a vast collection of my mother's recipes—in handwritten notebooks, yellowed with age, as some notes are over half a century old. I would also like to thank Shuchi, my bhabhi. She too mailed me some delicious recipes from friends who are well-known for their Lucknowi Khana skills.

Thanks to my cousin in New York, Ravi Trehan, who virtually grew up in our home (as did his brother, Karan, who were part of my brother's kaancha—marbles—brigade) for writing the note about his memories. Thanks to Seran, his wife, whose legendary hospitality in their homes in New York, Bedford and Cyprus is so much like the open hospitality of our parents' homes.

I would like to thank my WhatsApp Group of 'Loreto Girls Forever', the Class of '62 who are now spread across three continents: Kamal Sihota (who brought us all together and is much missed), Rita Lal (for creating this group), Bina Wadhwa, Chitra Sud, Gauri Dwivedi, Indira Baptista, Kiran Saxena, Meera Gupta, Mummo Khan, Nasima Faridi, Nilofer Qureshi, Nishat Hazratji, Rekha Agarwal, Sarita Behl, Sarita Chawla and Vandana Narain. They helped me remember the many dishes we ate and relished and the best eateries of Lucknow that we used to frequent.

My equal thanks to our many good friends in Lucknow who either cook or entertain or write insightful books on Lucknow and its cuisine: Dr Pushpesh Pant, a friend with a phenomenal knowledge about the art, culture and cuisine along the Silk Road. His books on this subject have been referred to with his permission. Parveen Talha, Veena Oldenberg and Nasima Faridi are all well-known authors on Lucknow. Jimmy Jahangirabad, Suleiman and Vijaya Mahmudabad and Shahila and Wajahat Habibullah sent me their traditional recipes. My thanks also to Zarine Viccajee, whose mother Zenobia was an excellent cook and exchanged many recipes with my mother.

Many thanks to my friend, Farzana Shahib, an excellent cook and skilled artist for her recipe of Karale ki Sabzi—the best I've ever tasted has been in her home. Kaneez Nargis Raza, fondly known as Nabaat, is a brilliant chef and shared her recipes of Murgh Mussalam, Noor Mehali Pulao and Patili Kebab.

My heartfelt thanks to David Davidar and Bena Sareen of Aleph Book Company for agreeing to publish this, my mother's second cookbook. This happened serendipitously whilst discussing another major book for which David has reposed more confidence in me than I have in myself! I also thank our editor, Pujitha Krishnan, who made many valuable suggestions.

The photography for this cookbook has been done by the talented Jasmer Singh. I am very grateful to Kohelika, our youngest daughter, who allowed me to convert her living room into Jasmer's photo studio for the duration of this week long shoot. I am also grateful to Kohelika for allowing me time off from our K2India Design Studio to enable me to work on her Nanima's cookbook.

As my mother had already written about four hundred recipes, from which hundred and fifty had to be selected for this book, I thought that the co-authoring of this book would be a simple task. Famous last words! My mother decided to re-examine every recipe and made several additions and deletions. As I told our publishers, writing is for professional writers. Apart from that, life gets in the way. This supposedly simple book took ten to twelve hours of continuous work for almost eight to ten weeks.

My grateful thanks to my assistant, Saachi Modgil, my amanuensis, who laboriously transcribed my handwritten pages into legible typescript, and for her many valuable inputs.

Thanks to my son, Suryaveer, for lending consistent support to his grandmother. He encouraged her to look at many more of her recipes, because of which this has become a more well-rounded cookbook.

Lastly, but most importantly, I thank my husband, Rome, for

showing exemplary patience when his wife refused invitations to all dinner parties and instead buried herself in her little 'book gazebo' in our courtyard.

~

Photo captions

pp. i and 220: Collection of Fatima's Hand in bronze used during Muharram.

p. ii: Gulaabpaash, used to sprinkle rosewater to welcome guests.

p. vi: Nineteenth-century English candleholders in silver.

p. xii: Phooldaan, a vase for holding flowers.

p. 226: Paandaan, a box for holding paan (betel leaf preparation).

p. 230: Late eighteenth-century itrdaan (perfume holder) in silver.

Recommended Reading

Ackerman, Diane, *A Natural History of the Senses*, Random House Inc, 1990.

Aijazuddin, F. S., *Lahore Recollected: An Album*, Sang-e-Meel Publications, 2003.

Allende, Isabel, *Aphrodite: A Memoir of the Senses*, Harper Perennial, 1999.

Baljekar, Mridula, *The Ultimate Indian Cookbook*, Om Book Service, 2007.

Banerji, Chitrita, *Eating India*, Penguin Books, 2008.

Bond, Ruskin and Saili, Ganesh, *Mussoorie & Landour: Days of Wine and Roses*, Roli Books, 2000.

Brennan, Jennifer, *Curries and Bugles: A Memoir and Cookbook of the British Raj*, Periplus, 2000.

Carrarini, Rose, *Breakfast, Lunch, Tea: The Many Little Meals of Rose Bakery*, Phaidon Press, 2005.

Chakravarty, Adity, *Reha'ish: At Home in Lucknow*, Sanatkada Publications.

Das, Neeta, *Architecture of Lucknow: Imambaras and Karbalas*, B. R. Publishing, 2008.

Feminists of Avadh Par Salaam!: Qisse, Yaadein aur Baatein, Sanatkada Publications, 2014.

Garten, Ina, foreword by Stewart, Martha, *The Barefoot Contessa Cookbook*, Clarkson Potter Publishers, 1999.

Goulding, Colonel H. R., *Old Lahore: Reminiscences of a Resident*, Sang-e-Meel Publications, 2007.

Graff, Violette, ed., *Lucknow: Memories of a City*, Oxford University Press, 1997.

Halim, Sharar Abdul, *Lucknow: The Last Phase of an Oriental Culture*, Paul Elek, 1975.

Hankin, Nigel B., *Hanklyn-Janklin*, Banyan Books, 1997.

Hay, Sidney, *Historic Lucknow*, The Pioneer Press, 1939.

Hickey, Ciaran, *Sultan's Table of the Turkish Cuisine*, Aksit, 2000.

Hosain, Attia, *Sunlight on a Broken Column*, Penguin Books, 2015.

Husain, Salma, *The Emperor's Table: The Art of Mughal Cuisine*, Roli Books, 2009.

———*Flavours of Avadh*, Niogi Books, 2015.

Hussain, Mirza Jafar, *Lucknow ka Dastarkhwan*, Urdu Academy, 2004.

Khurshid, Salman, *At Home in India: The Muslim Saga*, Hay House India, 2015.

Llewellyn-Jones, Rosie and Kidwai, Saleem, eds., *Hazratganj: A Journey through the Times*, Bennett Coleman & Co, 2011.

———*Last King in India: Wajid Ali Shah*, Random House India, 2014.

————ed. *Lucknow: City of Illusion*, Alkazi Collection of Photography, 2006.

Llewellyn-Jones, Rosie and Kapoor, Ravi, eds., *Lucknow, Then and Now*, Marg Publications, 2003.

Lucknow ki Rachi Basi Tehzeeb: The Making of a Cultural Mosaic, Sanatkada Publications, 2016.

Mack, John, *The Museum of the Mind: Art and Memory in World Culture*, The British Museum Press, 2003.

Manekshaw, Bhiku, *Feast of Love: 50 Classic Menus*, Penguin, 2007.

Markel, Stephen and Gude, Tushara Bindu, *India's Fabled City: The Art of Courtly Lucknow*, Del Monico Books, 2010.

Master Chefs of India, 1000 Great Indian Recipes—The Ultimate Book of Indian Cuisine, Roli Books, 2005.

Mathew, A. G., and Pushpanath, Salim, *Indian Spices*, Dee Bee Info Publications, 2005.

Misra, Amaresh, *Lucknow: Fire of Grace*, HarperCollins Publishers India, 1998.

Oldenburg, Veena Talwar, *The Making of Colonial Lucknow, 1856–1877*, Oxford University Press, 1990.

Ottolenghi, Yotam, *Plenty: Vibrant Vegetable Recipes from London's Ottolenghi*, Chronicle Books, 2011.

Paltrow, Gwyneth and Baumann, Thea, *It's All Easy: Delicious Weekday Recipes for the Super-Busy Home Cook*, Sphere, 2016.

Pande, Alka, *Mukhwas: Indian Food through the Ages*, ImprintOne, 2012.

Pant, Pushpesh, *Gourmet Journeys in India*, Roli Books, 2011.

————and Mohsin, Huma, *Food Path: Cuisine along the Grand Trunk Road from Kabul to Kolkata*, Roli Books, 2005.

Passmore, Jacki, *Asia: The Beautiful Cookbook*, Galley Press, 1992.

Raza, M. Hanif, *Lahore through Centuries*, Colorpix, 2000.

Rouff, Marcel, preface by Durrell, Lawrence, *The Passionate Epicure: La Vie et la Passion de Dodin-Bouffant, Gorumet*, The Modern Library, 2002.

Schimmel, Annemarie and Quraeshi, Samina, *Lahore: The City Within*, Concept Media, 1988.

Sen, Colleen Taylor, *Feasts and Fasts: A History of Food in India*, Speaking Tiger, 2016.

Sorensen, Felicia Wakwella, *The Exotic Tastes of Paradise: The Art of Sri Lankan Cooking*, Lincoln Green Publishing, 1989.

Steiner, Eliese, *The German Table*, Letterpress Design Studio, 2015.

Sur, Chand, *Continental Cooking for the Indian Palate*, Roli Books, 2003.

Swarup, Sushama, *Costumes and Textiles of Awadh: From the Era of Nawabs to Modern Times*, Roli Books, 2013.

Talha, Parveen, *Fida-e-Lucknow: Tales of the City and Its People*, Niyogi Books, 2013.

Tariq, Zubeida, *Zubeida Tariq's Kitchen*, Ferozsons, 2005.

Tyabji, Suraya, *Mirch Masala*, Orient Longman, 2002.

Vervoordt, May; Vermeulen Patrick and Gardner Michael, *At Home with May and Axel Vervoordt*, Random House Inc, 2012.

Vongerichten, Jean-Georges and Bittman, Mark, *Simple to Spectacular: How to Take One Basic Recipe to Four Levels of Sophistication*, Clarkson Potter, 2000.